Narratives of East Asian Women Teachers of English

NEW PERSPECTIVES ON LANGUAGE AND EDUCATION

***Series Editors*:** Professor Viv Edwards, *University of Reading, UK* and Professor Phan Le Ha, *University of Hawaii at Manoa, USA*

Two decades of research and development in language and literacy education have yielded a broad, multidisciplinary focus. Yet education systems face constant economic and technological change, with attendant issues of identity and power, community and culture. This series will feature critical and interpretive, disciplinary and multidisciplinary perspectives on teaching and learning, language and literacy in new times.

Full details of all the books in this series and of all our other publications can be found on http://www.multilingual-matters.com, or by writing to Multilingual Matters, St Nicholas House, 31-34 High Street, Bristol BS1 2AW, UK.

NEW PERSPECTIVES ON LANGUAGE AND EDUCATION: 57

Narratives of East Asian Women Teachers of English

Where Privilege Meets Marginalization

Gloria Park

MULTILINGUAL MATTERS
Bristol • Blue Ridge Summit

DOI 10.21832/PARK8729
Library of Congress Cataloging in Publication Data
A catalog record for this book is available from the Library of Congress.
Names: Park, Gloria G., - author.
Title: Narratives of East Asian Women Teachers of English: Where Privilege Meets Marginalization/Gloria Park.
Description: Bristol, UK; Blue Ridge Summit, PA: Multilingual Matters, [2017] | Series: New Perspectives on Language and Education: 57 | Includes bibliographical references and index.
Identifiers: LCCN 2017014948| ISBN 9781783098729 (hardcover: acid-free paper) | ISBN 9781783098736 (pdf) | ISBN 9781783098743 (epub) | ISBN 9781783098750 (kindle)
Subjects: LCSH: English language–Study and teaching (Higher)–Foreign speakers. | English language–Study and teaching–Social aspects. | English teachers–East Asia–Biography. | Women teachers–East Asia–Biography. | Park, Gloria G., 1967- | English teachers–United States–Biography. | Women teachers–United States–Biography.
Classification: LCC PE1128.A2 P3145 2017 | DDC 428.0071/05–dc23 LC record available at https://lccn.loc.gov/2017014948

British Library Cataloguing in Publication Data
A catalogue entry for this book is available from the British Library.

ISBN-13: 978-1-78309-872-9 (hbk)
ISBN-13: 978-1-78892-174-9 (pbk)

Multilingual Matters
UK: St Nicholas House, 31-34 High Street, Bristol BS1 2AW, UK.
USA: NBN, Blue Ridge Summit, PA, USA.

Website: www.multilingual-matters.com
Twitter: Multi_Ling_Mat
Facebook: https://www.facebook.com/multilingualmatters
Blog: www.channelviewpublications.wordpress.com

Copyright © 2017 Gloria Park.

All rights reserved. No part of this work may be reproduced in any form or by any means without permission in writing from the publisher.

The policy of Multilingual Matters/Channel View Publications is to use papers that are natural, renewable and recyclable products, made from wood grown in sustainable forests. In the manufacturing process of our books, and to further support our policy, preference is given to printers that have FSC and PEFC Chain of Custody certification. The FSC and/or PEFC logos will appear on those books where full certification has been granted to the printer concerned.

Typeset by Deanta Global Publishing Services Limited.
Printed and bound in the UK by the CPI Books Group Ltd.
Printed and bound in the US by Thomson-Shore, Inc.

Mom and Dad, Jong Im Lee and So Kwang Park, for sacrificing your lives for your children;

Han Nah, Liu, Xia, Yu Ri, and Shu-Ming for providing me access to your stories;

Jenny, Julie, and Michelle for "sistering" me when I need(ed) it the most;

Kevin and Aidan for giving me unconditional love and support in penning this book

Contents

	Acknowledgements	ix
	Prologue: (Re)Making the Book: Where Privilege and Marginalization Began	xiii
1	Rendering My Autobiographical Poetic Inquiry	1
2	Exposing our Discourses of Privilege and Marginalization: Gender, Race and Class Connections to Teaching English	11
3	'Writing *is* a Way of Knowing' in Promoting Evocative-Genres of Inquiry: Methodological Choices	29
4	Where Privilege Meets Marginalization in Han Nah's Lived Experiences: Navigating her Multiple Gendered Identities	44
5	Where Privilege Meets Marginalization in the Narratives of Liu, Xia and Yu Ri: Exploring Their Linguistic and Teacher Identities	60
6	Epilogue: Juxtaposing My Autobiographical Critical Incidents with Meanings gleaned from the Women's Narratives: Where Privilege Meets Marginalization	94
	Appendix A Guidelines for Electronic Reflective Autobiographical Narratives	104
	Appendix B Guidelines for Electronically Journaling Educational Incidents	107
	Appendix C Interview Questions	109
	References	111
	Index	121

Acknowledgements

Completing my book would not have been possible without the constant encouragement, support, and love from both my family, friends, professional colleagues, and most importantly, from my research partners.

I am forever beholden to Han Nah, Liu, Xia, Yu Ri, and Shu-Ming. At the time of completing this book, everyone is in the United States except for Yu Ri. Han Nah is a full time faculty at a university in East Coast upon completing her PhD in 2015, Liu and Xia are teaching ESOL in public school systems. They are both married with one child each. Shu-Ming teaches at a local community college and is married. Yu Ri is teaching English in Korea.

In addition to the five women who have made this book possible, I am grateful for my professors and mentors from University of Maryland, College Park (UMCP), with whom I have kept in touch. I am forever grateful to Francine Hultgren for her dedicated time to meet with me to catch up on our ups and downs. I am blessed to have Debra Suarez in my life for her mentorship and friendship, ultimately saving me and giving me the courage to stand up to my professorial bully. I would not be a seasoned teacher scholar without the mentoring from Bruce VanSledright, Jeremy Price, Suhanthie Motha, Elizabeth Marshall, Ryuko Kubota, Manka Varghese, and Margo DelliCarpini from whom I have gained much knowledge about critical and feminist pedagogies. They have all molded me in doing the work I am doing now, especially in continuing to wrestle with what it means to promote social justice issues in my own teacher scholarship.

Just as the aforementioned mentors and colleagues have nurtured me to be where I am, I thank my new family at Indiana University of Pennsylvania. Most importantly, I am grateful for the Sabbatical Research Leave (Spring 2016) awarded from my institution giving me ample time to complete most of the writing. While I missed teaching and interacting with my students, I needed daily writing time to complete this book. I am grateful to Marissa McKinley and Kelsey Hixson-Bowles for being my virtual writing buddies during my sabbatical. Furthermore, I am thankful for my colleagues and friends, Yaw Asamoah, Dan Tannacito, Chauna Craig, Curtis Porter, David Hanauer, Yi Yu, Ben Rafoth, Sharon Deckert, Gian Pagnucci and others that have championed my work and cheered me on to complete this book. I am also grateful for my dissertation students patiently waiting for me to return from my sabbatical so that they can complete their work. They have graciously given me space to work on my own writing. And to Dean Yaw Asamoah for supporting me in finding capable editorial and technical assistants, Kelsey Hixson-Bowles and Roger Powell. In addition to my

IUP family, I am grateful to the editors of the following journals for giving me permission to re-publish parts of my work: *TESOL Quarterly, L2 Journal, ELT Journal, Journal of Language, Identity and Education,* and *Race, Ethnicity and Education*. More importantly, I thank the editors who worked indefatigably with me to publish these original pieces, thus allowing my work and voice to shine.

The Multilingual Matters family has been a gem in guiding me in making a critical decision about signing my contract all the way to various points throughout the production of the book. I am forever grateful to both Viv Edwards and Phan Le Ha for their initial readings of my manuscript. My deep appreciation goes to Anna Roderick for being ever so patient and believing in me to complete this humongous project even when I was out of energy and patience. Furthermore, I appreciate the professional assistance and friendly encouragement from Florence McClelland, Laura Longworth and Sarah Williams in selecting my front book cover, deciding on marketing ideas, and completing different editorial stages.

I am blessed with a circle of friends, who believe in me and to whom I can vent about almost everything – Thank you, Sherrie Carroll, Kara Blank Gonzalez, Su Motha! Of course, I am even more blessed to have a large family who has championed me in many ways than I can verbalize on this page: I thank the two Moms in my life: One who gave birth to me, and one who gave birth to my better half. To my Dad, who has left us too early, but knowing that he is always watching over me and my family even from his peaceful home in heaven. I appreciate the visits from Paul and Genie O'Donnell and always opening their Florida and Tarpon Springs homes to us as places for respite. I am blessed to have found my 'New Jersey Mom and Dad', Rich and Kathy Spoerl, who continue to inspire me with their dedication to their grandchildren.

All the more, my extended family has always been my tenacious support from the day I was born. Uncle Jong Yul and Aunt Jung Ja, thank you for helping me understand the true meaning of family legacy and the roles of the eldest. Uncle Keun Hwan and Aunt Jong Sook, thank you for raising me as your daughter in my earlier years. Uncle Jong Yun and Aunt Grace, thank you for inviting us to live with you when we first immigrated to the US and giving us 'English' names so that we wouldn't be bullied for having 'unpronounceable' names. Uncle Jong Il and Aunt Hae Ja, thank you for showing me what it means to have strong work ethics in the midst of challenging times. Most importantly, Grandpa Jong Nam and Grandma Sun Yea, thank you for the chance to be the first in my own family to graduate from college and complete my doctoral education all because you two have decided to embark on your journey as new immigrants in the US in the early 1960s. My siblings and cousins, Michael and Julie, Jenny and James, Michelle and Kevin, Willy and Michelle, Ricky and Jae Eun, Jane and Yong,

Kris and Karin, Dennis and Ji Eun, Robert and Ji Hyun, Minna and Peter, Mark and Cheryl, and Oliver and Heather, thank you for allowing me the space to shine and succeed and making time to continue with our family legacy by getting our children's generation to understand the true meaning of family and support for one another.

Finally and most importantly, I am most privileged to be part of a loving and supportive family with Kevin O'Donnell and our son, Aidan Park O'Donnell. All in all, both have continued to champion me in completing my book and setting up a small but cozy writing space in our home for me to engage in my daily writing ritual. Even during the most difficult times, my husband and son knew exactly what to say to cheer me on and lift me up to fight both my inner and outer demons that continue to haunt me. Without my husband, Kevin, I don't think I would have completed my dissertation, a decade earlier, and now this book. Equally, my son has written alongside me during my Sabbatical to show me that we can both keep going with our passion of writing stories and constructing our identity as writers. I am indeed blessed and grateful.

Gloria Park
Rockville, Maryland
May 26, 2017

Prologue: (Re)Making the Book: Where Privilege and Marginalization Began

The seeds of this book were initially planted in 2000 when I started my doctoral studies at the University of Maryland, College Park. Throughout my coursework and dissertation research (2000–2006) with the five women highlighted in this book (Han Nah Jung, Liu Li, Xia Wang, Yu Ri Koh and Shu-Ming Fung),[1] I came to learn more about myself. Specifically, the epistemological and ontological perspectives on our fluid, multiple and contested identities traversing multiple contexts as women teachers of English became clearer as I delved deeper into our lives and the readings that guided this inquiry. My received and subjective knowledge was fine-tuned as I began putting all my ideas into writing this book (Belenky et al., 1997). In particular, listening to the voices of Han Nah, Liu, Xia, Yu Ri and Shu-Ming became a quest for self – my becoming an advocate for myself and other women in our journeys. This path to advocacy that I have journeyed through focuses on understanding how issues of privilege and marginalization intersect for myself and the five women as we traversed different contexts of teaching English. This book is unconventional in its genres compared to most of the academic books published in the field. My development of Self in relation to understanding of the Other (Phan, 2008) has been accomplished through writing personal narratives juxtaposed with my understanding of the literature and how those inform the ways in which I interpret the women's stories (Vandrick, 2009) of teaching English.

I now return to the earlier days of meeting each woman, followed by my critical reflections on the lessons learned from the women's lived experiences. Next, I share my researcher subjectivity, our commitment in my penning of the book, a brief note on privileging certain constructs and discourses throughout the book. I conclude with the organization of the book.

Earlier Days of Our Encounters: Introducing the Women

Bringing together our stories (Han Nah, Xia, Liu, Yu Ri, Shu-Ming and Gloria) did not commence until 2003, which was when I met Xia and Liu. In 2004, via professional colleagues, I met Han Nah, Yu Ri and Shu-Ming. These narrative snapshots serve as a brief introduction to the women.

Han Nah Jung

In October 2004, I met Han Nah through one of my colleagues at Atlantic University. Her interest in my focus on women's issues drew her into the study. Her research background in Turkish women's issues provided her with the rationale to participate. I was more than thrilled to have someone like Han Nah in my study. This stemmed from the fact that she would not only bring a wealth of gendered research experience into my study but would also bring her gendered experiences as a wife and a mother.

Han Nah Jung, a native of South Korea, was born in 1970 in a suburb near Seoul. She graduated from one of Korea's leading universities in 1992, where she majored in Turkish and Islamic Women's studies. She also did short-term studies in Turkey, England and the US (1992–1994), before getting married in 1995. Her husband's desire to obtain a higher education brought Han Nah to New York in 1996. She began taking intensive English language courses until she became pregnant and had to be homebound due to childcare considerations. When her husband completed his master's degree program and his visa status changed to full-time international employee, Han Nah's visa status changed as well.

In 2001, Han Nah's G4 visa allowed her to establish a working status in the US. This opened up many possibilities for Han Nah, including teaching the Korean language at an institution of higher education and at a private language institute, and beginning her Teaching English to Speakers of Other Languages (TESOL) program. Han Nah stated that as long as her husband held his position at his current international organization, she would be content to remain in the US, pursue her PhD and start a bilingual school for Korean-American children. Hence, Han Nah stated the following as her ultimate goal for matriculating in a TESOL program:

> [English] was my minor, and it is really important language in Korea. … And then, the second one is that my children are bilingual, so I am always thinking about how I can teach them both Korean and English at the same time. Then, it led me to start learning English education, TESOL, kind of teaching language.

Liu Li

In September 2003, I first came into contact with Liu through a mutual academic acquaintance. In the beginning of our interactions, she struck me as reserved, but was very much willing to share with me things that have been bothering her on a variety of topics. These included her program, her classes and her life as a married woman pursuing higher education in the US while her husband remained in China. My desire to understand her educational experiences in China and in the US led me to invite her into my study, and our conversations began in October 2004.

In 1978, Liu Li was born in a town called Datong, a suburb of Beijing in China. In July 2003, two months after taking her marital vows, and after having wrestled with the US visa system, she landed in the US to embark on her TESOL master's degree program. This required that she leave her husband behind to attend to his self-owned business in China. Initially, she was planning to pursue her PhD in the US after completing her master's program in TESOL, but she decided to put that on hold and return to China to be with her husband and family upon completion of her master's program in December 2005. Her goals for entering the US TESOL program were as follows:

> I am interested in learning the English language. The longer I study this language I feel I take more responsibility to introduce this beautiful language to as many people as possible [in China]. Therefore, I entered the TESOL program to learn how to teach it effectively.

Xia Wang

Xia made her feelings of linguistic powerlessness evident during one of our initial encounters in September 2003, which was set up through one of our mutual colleagues. I became interested in Xia and wanted to know more about her views and what made her feel so powerless. In December 2004, when I formally began my data collection, she reiterated those words of feeling powerless due to her lack of English language proficiency. She linked it to her status as a temporary resident in the US.

Xia is a native of China, born in Beijing in 1979. She had been immersed in the Chinese educational system from 1985 until she began her master's in European studies in Germany in 2002. When she was admitted into the school in Germany, she was also given a full fellowship to begin a master's in TESOL program at Pacific University in the US. Xia's desire to be with her boyfriend pushed her away from Pacific University and into commencing her program in Germany; as a result, she deferred her fellowship opportunity at Pacific University until September 2003. At the time of my study (2004–2005), she was finishing up her master's in TESOL at Pacific University. Even though she was not planning to teach in a pre-K–12 English as a second language (ESL) context, she had decided to take the TESOL state licensure track in order to better understand the public school system in the US. Hence, during the spring of 2005, she completed her student teaching as a partial requirement for her master's in TESOL K–12 certification track. Xia shared, 'Instead of being a classroom teacher and affecting a class of students, I'd like to improve English teaching and learning in China by developing more effective and engaging teaching materials' (Xia, E-Auto Narrative, 2004).

Yu Ri Koh

In October 2004, I met Yu Ri for the first time through one of my academic acquaintances. Her youth, liveliness and willingness to participate in my study were more than desirable. She was very humble in stating that she did not know whether she could truly contribute to my study.

Yu Ri was born in Seoul, Korea, in 1980. During her middle school years, she had had the opportunity to come to the US for one year (1992–1993) because her father was given a student fellowship at one of the universities in New York. While studying English in New York as a middle school student, she became enamored with the idea of learning English as a tool for communication, as opposed to studying it to pass exams in Korea. Yu Ri's stay in New York provided her with an initial opening into the world of English language learning. She graduated from Ko Rya foreign language high school in 1999, with the hopes of entering one of the leading universities for women in Korea. Unfortunately, her dreams were shattered when she did not make the cut-off score for the leading women's university in Korea; thus, she entered her second choice in 1999, Yeo Ja University, located in a suburb of Seoul.

Since Yeo Ja University was not her first choice, she felt like a failure for having to study at this university. At the same time, she also desired to improve her English language skills and improve her understanding of world events. As a result, she decided to embark on an international transfer. She transferred from Yeo Ja University in Korea to Atlantic University in the US in 2001, with a junior standing in an undergraduate program in International Relations. Hoping to further improve her English language skills, in addition to wanting to know more about the English language teaching enterprise, she entered a master's in TESOL program at Atlantic University in 2003 directly from her undergraduate experience. She chose Atlantic University due to her familiarity with the campus and the TESOL program. Yu Ri commented, 'I have been interested in studying about English education since when I was a college student in Korea. I was especially interested in teaching English to kids' (Yu Ri, E-Auto Narrative, 2004).

Shu-Ming Fung

I initially hesitated to include Shu-Ming Fung in my study due to her lengthy residence in the US compared to the other women. However, her self-identification as a nonnative English speaker (NNES) and her multitude of complex identities made her an ideal candidate for the study. Her identities became more complex as she began to teach English and learn more about TESOL pedagogy. Her claiming dual identities as an NNES became evident in one of our early interviews in terms of how she saw herself vis-à-vis the others in her TESOL program (Aneja, 2016).

Shu-Ming Fung was born in 1970 in Taipei, Taiwan. She immigrated to this country with her family at the age of 13 in 1983, and began her education in the US as an eighth grader. At the time of my data collection (2004–2005), she was finishing up her master's in TESOL program at Atlantic University. Shu-Ming entered a college in the Mid-Atlantic region as a government politics major in 1988, and she was employed for 10 years (1991–2001) in a government printing company. During her third visit to Taiwan in 2001, her extended family members there encouraged her to tutor adults and children in English, as a way to gain some cultural experience and economic viability. From 2001 to 2003, she tutored in Taiwan. She felt the need to improve her methods of teaching English and desired to find a credible teacher education program to pursue this course of action. After researching on the internet for different programs in both the US and England, she found the Atlantic University TESOL program, located in the Mid-Atlantic region.

In spring 2003, upon returning from her two-year tutoring venture in Taiwan, she commenced her master's in TESOL program. In tandem with her TESOL program, Shu-Ming began a volunteer teaching job in an adult ESL program in a nearby county. Specifically, she taught survival English and citizenship classes to newly arrived immigrants, refugees and asylum seekers from all over the world, but predominantly from Southeast Asian and African countries. She saw herself as a linguistic and cultural resource for her students. With the goal of improving her pedagogical practices, Shu-Ming shared the following: 'I came into TESOL because I knew I was a terrible tutor of English [in Taiwan]. I enjoyed tutoring/teaching English, but I did not know how to do it effectively' (Shu-Ming, E-Auto Narrative, 2004).

Reflecting on Lessons Learned from Our Lived Experiences

As a teacher and researcher educator, I often reflect on the lessons learned from the women and their experiences. Liu, Xia and Yu Ri have guided me in my work as a teacher educator and the meanings of being and becoming language teachers. Both Liu and Xia became enamored by their mentor teachers' care and commitment toward their profession as teachers of English as an additional language (EAL) students. They realized that teaching EAL is more than performing perfect English, but really caring about their students and their academic as well as emotional needs. Moreover, Yu Ri's constant comparison of her student teaching experience in a US high school has helped her to be critical of the education she received in South Korea, together with her realization that the high school students she interacted with in the US *do* care about their educational trajectory. I often point out to my student teachers how Liu, Xia and Yu Ri navigated their experiences of classroom management and their work with mentor teachers and students. It is in these moments that I, too, reflect on my current pedagogical practices.

Our stories are interconnected in many ways as we journeyed through the English language learning and teaching landscapes in our native countries as well as in the US TESOL programs. As a Korean immigrant woman, I had always felt that my stories of hybridity were unique but static, and often problematically interpreted – that I could be both a native and a non-native speaker of English. Throughout penning this book, I became more aware of the (dis)connection between these linguistic identities, and how others perceived me and how I perceived myself. Specifically, one of these moments of (dis)connectedness was with Shu-Ming. Shu-Ming's experiences of navigating her (non)native speaking (Aneja, 2016) illustrate confidence and a higher level of commitment toward her work with EAL students. I am not saying that I don't show commitment to my field. However, Shu-Ming engaged in 'volunteer teaching' for a couple of years before getting paid and having her own class. This shows a deep commitment that is rarely seen in teachers (Nieto, 2004). Moreover, when I juxtapose my own autobiography with that of Shu-Ming, I come to understand how I perceive my own linguistic and teacher identities. Through intimate conversations with Shu-Ming, I am reminded of our shifting identities and how we position one another, given the various roles we play in our social and professional communities. This is the story I am choosing to tell about how I perceive Shu-Ming, and how I perceive myself vis-à-vis Shu-Ming. Shu-Ming may have a different version of this story, but it is within this story constructed by me that I understand my teacher identity.

There are many similarities between Shu-Ming and I, but also many differences, hence the '(dis)connectedness'. For instance, we both immigrated to the US during our childhood; we both fell into teaching English, even though it was not part of our post-secondary disciplinary major; we both returned to our native countries to teach English; we returned to the US to gain credentials in teaching English at the same institution (but in different cohorts), which focused on promoting a communicative teaching philosophy; we developed our emerging teacher identities at the same community college's pre-academic English language program; and we both love and are committed to teaching English. On the personal level, we are both married to Caucasian men, though their educational backgrounds and social classes differ. While I have a biological son, Shu-Ming has a 'son', her sister's son whom she has been taking care of for as long as I have known her. While we love spending time with our respective families, we privilege our work and teaching (I think) more often than not. In terms of professional and educational pursuits, I have continued with my education beyond my MATESOL degree, and am a practicing teacher educator in MA/PhD programs in a higher education institution. I am currently on sabbatical writing my first book, as well as teaching one academic writing course at the same institution where Shu-Ming teaches. I see Shu-Ming on a regular basis and she continues to develop professionally via teaching and facilitating special projects at the community college.

The reason I share these details is because I don't have the same level of (dis)connectedness with the other women in my book. I do share some with Han Nah, but not to the point of comparing myself and seeing my reflections of teacher identity (or lack thereof) and thinking what I could do to be as confident as I perceive her to be. This critical reflection has guided me in exploring how the 2006 snapshots of our teacher identity narratives coincide with those of the 2017 narrative snapshots. This means committing to additional interview time with Shu-Ming, and as long as Shu-Ming consents, a journal manuscript will focus on this decade of teacher identity transformation (2006–2016) on Shu-Ming and myself. In many ways, this additional research project will allow me the space to entertain the (dis)connectedness I feel and live with on a daily basis, as Shu-Ming and I explore our decade of teacher identities in-the-making. I certainly do not want to short-change the feeling that emanates when I reread Shu-Ming's interview data from 2006 and how I see her now in the community college contexts. As such, I feel more strongly about an entirely different scholarly venue for privileging Shu-Ming's life history and how my own interlaces.

Additionally, in reflecting on privilege and marginalization coexistence, I note the differences between Shu-Ming and the rest of the women. First, the forms of privilege that described Han Nah, Liu, Xia and Yu Ri did not exist for Shu-Ming. For example, Shu-Ming did not attend English conversation classes in Taiwan or do any study abroad programs outside of Taiwan. These were unique for the international NNESs in the study. The women in the study, other than Shu-Ming, could be labeled as the Global Elites that Vandrick (2011) referred to in her *TESOL Quarterly* article, who come to the US with much capital that would sustain them throughout their education. However, her family's migration to the US could be seen as a form of privilege, since they were exposed to different forms of capital, which would not have been available to them in Taiwan. The very nature of the interaction with the English language plus learning and teaching in the ESL context gave Shu-Ming privileges that she would not have received if her family had stayed in Taiwan. In general, Shu-Ming came from a different social-class background compared to the international NNESs in the study.

Second, Shu-Ming's length of stay in the US, coupled with the commencement of her ESL experience at an early age, gave her more access to academic socialization in terms of navigating the schooling process compared to the rest of the women. These enabled her to be confident in navigating the social languages embedded in both the academic and social contexts (Gee, 2004). Also, Shu-Ming embraced her fluid and transnational identities of NNES and near-NES and perceived her identities as more of an asset than a liability in most situations, unlike the other women. As a result, she saw herself being able to accomplish more with her fluid and shifting identities throughout her educational and teaching experiences, especially as a TESOL graduate student and an ESL teacher.

Finally, Shu-Ming envisioned a different set of imagined future possibilities for herself. She envisioned herself being able to teach English in both the US and some East Asian countries (i.e. China, Taiwan and Japan). In particular, she was able to claim a transnational identity, being able to go from one linguistic and cultural context to another with very few perceived challenges with respect to her teaching abilities. The other women in the study did not believe that it would be possible to obtain appropriate teaching positions in their native countries due to the dominant discourse privileging native English speakers (NESs) from English-speaking countries as teachers. This ideological mindset regarding who is seen as a more credible English teacher around the world was already ingrained in the experiences of Han Nah, Liu, Xia and Yu Ri since they had access to NESs within and beyond their home countries throughout their early educational processes. However, toward the end of her TESOL program, Shu-Ming did find out that she would encounter some foreseeable obstacles in finding a teaching position in China due to her national and political identities as a Taiwanese woman. Shu-Ming stated that there were some political implications in hiring a native of Taiwan.

Rendering my Researcher Subjectivity

While this book started out as a focus on the five women who were gracious enough to share their experiences throughout the writing of my dissertation, I cannot minimize what I have learned from the women who entered my life for they are part of my subjective experiences. As such, documenting our lived experiences in multiple contexts continues to complicate our identities of race, gender, class and language. In particular, how dominant ideology and discourses surface as non-white NNESs in the US became a constant reawakening in my pursuit of justice in our lives. I am reminded of Ladson-Billings' (2000: 268) powerful statement that this line of research inevitably relates to a search into negotiating my (de)/(re)constructed identities for how these experiences 'affect what, how, and why I research' the women. Therefore, my research interest and my life as a minority woman and researcher have and will continue to intersect; these influences are the multiple lenses I bring into my inquiry. Specifically, this book focuses on the lives of six women teachers of English in general and, in particular, how our lives are complicated by English and its privilege and marginalization. Throughout my writing of this book, I have come to think more deeply about each woman and her stories of experience. While my goal is not to privilege certain stories over others, I am conscious about my own critical reflections on each woman and her TESOL professional journey.

Writing this book has been both psychological and scholarly. It is psychological in that I reflect on my identities vis-à-vis each woman. Each woman teaches me something about myself and my development of teacher identity. It is also therapeutic, in that I can be more forthcoming about the transitional phase of my identities as a mama scholar. Being honest with myself and sharing this understanding of self is what makes penning this book so liberating. Within this therapeutic mechanism lies the questioning aspect of writing this book as a woman of color academician: *Am I falling into the hegemonic practice of publish or perish? Why can't I let this book go? Why is it important to tell our stories as women teachers of English?* I realize that there is no one answer to these lingering questions. The responses are complex, since they have to do with English language and its impact in the worldwide contexts; how our home countries and the educational policies enacted are (dis)connected with the global push for Englishization; how our identities are being continuously shaped as a result of this global push; how the US TESOL programs are continuing to produce teachers who challenge and perpetuate dominant discourses in our profession; and how we as English teachers have weathered through these moments.

Our Commitment and the Goals of This Book

The goals of this book are illustrated in our commitment. As a teacher, teacher educator and researcher from an East Asian background myself, I wanted to know and understand our driving forces in seeking out US TESOL programs. For all of us, to a certain degree, English was and is a symbol of power and privilege, a symbol of educational access and a pursuit of equity, and yet at times a symbol of linguistic marginalization. As such, each woman had a specific rationale for seeking out admission into her US TESOL program, and each woman, in her own way, sought to access power and privilege in positioning herself in a way that would empower her teacher and linguistic identities.

Han Nah wanted to be in a community where she could live out her gendered identity as a mother, providing instruction to her children bilingually while also staking a claim to a professional teaching identity that would involve teaching an important language in Korea, yet deciding to teach her dominant language in the US. In the cases of Liu, Xia and Yu Ri, they wanted to be a part of a professional teaching community by being a language and cultural broker, teaching children and being an effective pedagogue, respectively. Through their student teaching experiences, they came to better understand their roles and identities as TESOL teachers. As for Shu-Ming, her optimism toward her linguistic and teacher identities became a role model for my own journey. Henceforth, our stories reveal complex relationships, where privilege and marginalization coexist and cut across our perceived and assigned identities of race, gender, social class and language. This complex coexistence centered on how the English language becomes a powerful conduit in our identity (de)/(re)constructions and negotiations.

While understanding our rationale for embarking on the US TESOL programs became a critical goal of this book, our commitment is also to serve as advocates for one another in our field. I am committed to my students, who come from all walks of life. However, I am also committed to junior (women) colleagues in my field, especially those at my institution who are wrestling with motherhood in the academy, as is the case for me (Castaneda & Isgro, 2013; Evans & Grant, 2008). My work with the five women is an extension of who I am. Juxtaposing our lived experiences as students, teachers, professionals, daughters, spouses and moms (for some of us) has helped me to further my research endeavor in writing about the complexities at the core of who I am as a minority woman, mother in the academy, spouse and teacher educator. Being a new mom in the academy was a challenging yet worthwhile endeavor. While Han Nah, one of my research partners, delineated her mothering identity early on in my inquiry, my own did not emerge until I started my tenure-track position with three-month-old Aidan in my arms and my spouse accompanying the move to Western Pennsylvania. As such, the (re)making of this book in 2017 is more thought provoking and richer now than it would have been several years ago, due to the inclusion of my own lived experiences navigating the multiple identities that have molded and will continue to mold me. In addition, I can articulate clearly the ways in which I think about who I am, who I have become and what my imagined identities might be vis-à-vis exploring the women's narratives. As such, I inject my critical reflections throughout the restorying of the women's narratives, which I was not able to do freely before writing this book.

The next goals are related to the aforementioned ones. By sharing our lived experiences, I desire to document the discourses of privilege and marginalization that point to the interlocking system of structural (in) equity in our (lived) experiences as women teachers of English. As such, this book is about how the six of us experienced our lives in the midst of our desire to overcome the challenging and empowering nature of the English language. This book is about sharing who we are as transnational and mobile women living in the midst of linguistic privilege and marginalization.

Finally, documenting our lived experiences embodies our teacher-scholar identity. In particular, this book illustrates what I have learned from the women, and how lessons learned from these women's stories have shaped my TESOL practice. This book is about coming to know who I am and who I have become as a language educator, woman scholar, mama scholar and writer. This book is also about my relationship with each woman – how I have matured professionally as a result of lessons learned from their lives as TESOL professionals. This book is, most importantly, about our love and hate of the English language and the ways in which it (dis)empowers us.

A Brief Note on Privileging Certain Constructs and Discourses

Throughout this book, I privilege certain constructs and discourses that attempt to liberate our multiple identities and celebrate our lived histories. The list is exhaustive, but I point out a couple of examples that illustrate my perspectives. For instance, instead of using English language learners (ELLs) or English as a second/foreign language (ESL/EFL), I promote the use of English as an additional language (EAL) or English as an international language (EIL) to students as much as possible, in order to remind ourselves that English is used by everyone and that we do not have to be labeled as learners. Furthermore, by privileging EAL as a form of additional linguistic repertoire, I am making a conscious choice to 'erase' the power inherent in who is perceived as an ideal (English) language learner. Equally important is the ideology of dismantling the hierarchical nature of English within individuals' linguistic repertoires. Yet, I prefer to leave certain constructs used by scholars in the literature being cited as they are. An example of this would be the use of NNESs and NESs. Although the core of this book combats these dichotomous perspectives, I also need to point out the ways in which these constructs are being used in the scholarship. The meaning behind privileging certain constructs over others has much to do with issues of power, privilege and status (or lack thereof) that come with the English language and its speakers.

Organization of the Book

This book is a beginning of my life's work. As such, certain chapters have been reworked from my publications. However, there is also a lot of new writing included in this book. The new writings are part of the Prologue, Chapter 2, Chapter 3, Chapter 5 and Chapter 6. The following is a brief overview of each chapter.

In this prologue, I have introduced the women and my relationship with each one as one way to document how penning this book began. A brief introduction to each woman foreshadows the later chapters focusing on Han Nah, Liu, Xia and Yu Ri. As stated earlier, I have earmarked my interlacing of Shu-Ming's and my transformative teacher identities, chronicling a decade of possibilities in an (auto)-ethnographic poetic inquiry for a journal article; yet, I do include Shu-Ming and her narratives throughout the book as deemed appropriate. While I do not have a chapter dedicated to Shu-Ming's narrative, she is very much an important part of making this book and guiding me to be critically reflective about my own identities-in-the-making in the past decade and in the years to come. In addition, I have reflected on the lessons learned from our lived experiences so as to further discuss my relationships with the women and how those relationships guided my practice and identities. I shared my researcher subjectivity, and I explicated our commitment to our field by discussing the goals of this book. I concluded with a brief note about privileging certain constructs and discourses throughout this book.

In Chapter 1: Rendering My Autobiographical Poetic Inquiry, I foreground my own story as an autobiographical-poetic inquiry. In working with and writing about women's life histories, it was only fair to share my stories with each woman. While the poetic inquiry was composed much later in our journeys, bits and pieces of my history were shared with them throughout our dialogic inquiry. As such, (re)interpreting my life history and critically reflecting on my own identity transformation also occurred throughout our dialogic inquiry.

In Chapter 2: Exposing our Discourses of Privilege and Marginalization: Gender, Race and Class Connections to Teaching English, I briefly focus on the literature discussing the gender, race and class connections in teaching English, which further exposes how discourses of privilege and marginalization have influenced our lives. I argue that socially and discursively constructed gendered identities, coupled with racialized and classed discourses, have continued to (re)shape our language teacher identities as transnational multilinguals. Moreover, I delineate some of the relevant scholarship on gender, race and class privilege connected to the women's lived experiences. I conclude the chapter by critiquing the perceived necessities and desire to earn an academic degree in the US as a way to discuss and problematize the English language educational policy issues in the women's home countries.

In Chapter 3: 'Writing *is* a Way of Knowing' in Promoting Evocative Genders of Inquiry: Methodological Choices, I outline the methodological lens that is at the heart of this book. This chapter serves as a methodology chapter. First, I claim my 'autobiographical self' as research instrument, in that my perspectives color the ways in which I interpret and restory our narratives. Next, I argue that the very lessons learned from constructing my autobiography have allowed me to understand who I have become as a teacher-scholar researcher, ultimately giving me a sense of identity to pen this book. I contend that being a reflexive and political researcher is a must in continuing to battle issues of power, privilege, marginalization and access that are intimately connected to writing our stories. As such, in order to promote the political stance that comes with writing about women's (and particularly women of color) experiences, I privilege narrative as a process of inquiry in making sense of our life events. In particular, I view evocative genres such as autobiography, life history and poetic inquiry, to name just a few, as forms of decolonizing methodological and pedagogical approaches, which is also consistent with my political perspectives on doing research on women. Finally, I conclude the chapter by claiming that our dialogic inquiry has helped me to practice our dialogical narrative of storytelling.

In Chapter 4: Where Privilege Meets Marginalization in Han Nah's Lived Experiences: Navigating her Multiple Gendered Identities, I highlight the ways in which I interpreted Han Nah's journey in wrestling with her multiple gendered identities. This chapter also focuses on how I began to make sense of the unfolding of my own lived experiences as a daughter, spouse, teacher educator and mama scholar in the academy. In particular, I attempt to entertain the question posed by the work of post-structuralists such as Judith Butler and Bonny Norton, 'how did gender come to make a difference?' in our lives as women traversing different contexts (Higgins, 2010: 373). Would we have had the same experiences if we were men? As such, I privilege gender as a lens to unfold our lived experiences, and I argue that 'women's experiences need to be understood not only at the institutional level but also at the personal level. Women's familial experiences are conditioned by the social and familial structure and are also related to their gendered desire' (Lee & Park, 2001).

In Chapter 5: Where Privilege Meets Marginalization in the Narratives of Liu, Xia and Yu Ri: Exploring Their Linguistic and Teacher Identities, I depict their engagement with English in their home countries, their experiences in working for professional companies, their experiences leading up to and being matriculated in US TESOL programs and their engagement with mentor teachers and students in (pre)student teaching experiences. As such, the dominant theme of their linguistic identities influencing their teacher identities and vice versa, and how these identities shifted from their native countries to the TESOL programs and ultimately to their newly established teaching communities, was central in the experiences of Liu, Xia and Yu Ri. Because this chapter includes the life events of three women, the organization of this particular chapter became important in delineating the shifts from one context to the next.

In Epilogue: Juxtaposing My Autobiographical Critical Incidents with Meanings gleaned from the Women's Narratives: Where Privilege Meets Marginalization, I move away from the traditional notion of writing a final chapter. In other words, I don't use the final chapter to delineate a summary of themes emerging from the book. I return to bits and pieces of my own autobiographical narratives in the making and my critical reflections of the world around me, especially in the wake of the 45th presidential inauguration and the Women's March in DC in January 2017. These autobiographical narratives illustrate critical incidents in my life as a woman and mama scholar in the academy. In turn, these narratives parallel the themes emerging from the (re)storying of Han Nah, Liu, Xia, Yu Ri and Shu-Ming, to highlight the coexistence of privilege and marginalization. My narrative depictions may seem like I am exposing certain individuals in the academy. However, it is not about those individuals, but the ideologies embedded in their discourses and identities. While I love the work I do at my institution and I adore the students with whom I work, I realize the need to be critical of my own actions and the environment in which I work. This concept of criticality is at the core of this final chapter. As such, in this chapter, I attempt to capture what it means to be critical, to raise critical consciousness around who we are, what we do and what we stand for and, ultimately, to know and reaffirm that there is power that comes with shared experiences across different but similar peoples in the academy. This is a reminder for me and for others that we are constantly wrestling with coexisting in both privileged and marginalized landscapes.

Note

(1) All names and institutions used in this book are pseudonyms, except for the author's name.

1 Rendering My Autobiographical Poetic Inquiry[1,2]

> *The notion that having greater consciousness of the spaces we inhabit and our relation to others may lead us to act more justly in the world is an appealing one, I admit, and one that has helped to shape my own teaching.*
> James, 2007: 161

James' (2007) reminder about 'acting justly in the world' rings true for me as I return to my own autobiography as well as the constructed narratives on the women. Personally, 'acting justly in the world' needs to begin with myself, in my research and pedagogy. It is only when I am critically conscious about my own lived/living experiences that I can begin to understand how to act more justly in my world, which ultimately affects others interacting with me. Being critically conscious also allows for me and other women to be mindful of relationships of power and privilege existing in our various contexts that shape our lives (Nussbaum, 1999 cited in James, 2007: 167). Building on the inquiry of Nussbaum (1999), James (2007) asks a series of questions that are just as vital in exploring our lived experiences in the writing of this book.

> Whose voices count? Who has access and whose access is limited? How do various cultural and institutional norms and discourses perpetuate these relationships of power? In what ways do individuals and groups enact agency to challenge these relationships? (James, 2007: 167–168)

To this end, this chapter illustrates my story of becoming and coming to know the various ways in which my identities have surfaced in my life, which became the foundation for understanding the lives of the women in this book.

The Poem: *Untitled*[3]

> *There is a garden*
> *Full of beautiful*
> *chrysanthemums*

Different colors
And heights
There is another garden

Full of red roses
As red as the loss of love
I have walked

The path between these
Two gardens
Sometimes I sit there for hours

Written about 30-something years ago, this *Untitled* poem has travelled with me from the summer of 1984, on a beautiful green acre campus, to 2012, on a cloudy day in December, in my office overlooking the barren trees that line the path between North and East Halls. And now, in 2017, it is part of writing this book. This poem is truly an act of identity (de)/(re) construction, a political act that is very much connected to the personal and the professional (Ayers, 2004; Freire, 1998; hooks, 2010; Hurlbert, 2012). It was in the act of trying to find myself, constructing and negotiating my identity in different spaces with different individuals, that I was able to write this poem. This poem is simple, yet meaningful. Some would argue that autobiographical creative writing is meaningful for everyone. I further argue that my autobiography, layered in poetic discourses constructed around the 'epistemological principle of the unique … provides its readers with specific insights into individual, personal human experience and linguistic expression' (Hanauer, 2003: 69), embodies who I am. Then and now, I do know that writing, specifically writing in English as an additional language (EAL), has a critical place in my life as a language learner, language teacher and teacher/researcher educator in teaching English to speakers of other languages (TESOL). Writing in EAL continues to impact me as I pen this book.

Depending on where I am and what my roles are, *Untitled*, written in 1984, provides me with a sense of belonging and, at the same time, a sense of uncoupling in the midst of my divided world, as depicted in two renditions written in 2013 in the making of the original *L2 Journal* article. While the poetic words were written in my own reflections, I can't help but think about how the (lived) experiences of Han Nah, Liu, Xia, Yu Ri and Shu-Ming could also be critical components of this poetic inquiry. As such, revisiting this poetic inquiry is dedicated to our lives and the ways in which we have come thus far.

As a result of my lived experiences, I privilege discourses and pedagogies that unveil my attributes as one way to humanize what I do as a teacher educator preparing teachers to teach EAL (Bartolomé, 2009). Just as it is important for me to note my lack of white privilege, it is also vital that the women and I acknowledge how both privilege and marginalization coexist in our journeys as (English) teachers. As such, this autobiographic-poetic inquiry is NOT a victimized narrative (Motha, 2006). It is a detailed account of how I (perhaps as well as other women in similar situations) navigate the coexistence of privilege and marginalization.

I highlight four distinct but interconnected areas of my life history that I refer to as *autobiographic poetic waves*. These waves are layered with the complex underpinning of racial, linguistic, gendered, classed and professional identity politics that continue to not only liberate, but also subjugate me at times; thus I am constantly living in a state of contradiction. Ultimately, the contents of these autobiographic poetic waves reveal being critically conscious of the identity politics of individuals from (dis)enfranchised spaces. As much as these (auto)biographic poetic waves represent my lived experiences, they also speak in relation to the lived experiences of Han Nah, Liu, Xia, Yu Ri and Shu-Ming. While moving away from an essentialized understanding of women, especially women from East Asian countries, it is important to point out shared stories of critical incidents that have (dis) empowered us as (non)native-speakered women teachers of English (Aneja, 2016). It is our overlapping identities of race, gender, class and language that allow us to find peace in sharing our stories. As argued by Hanauer (2012), the rendering of my autobiographic poetic waves is in itself part of a (de)/(re)construction of my meaningful literacy, which embodies my multiple, ever-changing and contradictory identity options. Discussion of these waves is interspersed with the extended version of *Untitled* written in 1984. This poetic rendering was a necessarily challenging and liberating step while (re)constructing the stories of the five women.

Autobiographic Poetic Wave One: Immigration and the Emergence of Hyphenated Identities

A garden full of beautiful chrysanthemums
Different colors and heights
An adventurous new beginning
Full of hope and promise for better education
Maintaining Korean at home
Learning English at school

Another garden full of red roses
As red as the loss of love
Culturally irrelevant curriculum
Being the only visible minority
Without English language knowledge
Wounded by series of name calling[4]

Although immigration is perceived as an act of adventure, a new beginning of one's life in a land of promise and prosperity, I came to experience my emigration from Korea as a disenfranchised experience in the English-speaking world. My coming to the US at an early age was unlike that of the children in the 'geese family (gerogi gajok)' depicted in the early study abroad programs, where mothers and children come to English-speaking countries (most often to the US) for the children to embark on a US educational journey, while fathers stay in South Korea to finance the transnational educational endeavors (Shin, 2014; Song, 2011). Moreover, my immigration, perhaps similar to that of Shu-Ming and her family's emigration from Taiwan, was different from other women's transnational moves. At least, except for Shu-Ming, the women knew some English, and the transnational adventure was an option as part of their educational pursuits.

The white teachers whom I encountered in 1976 did not, or perhaps could not, relate to me, though they comforted me in their arms whenever I shed tears of frustration and anger. I did not think anyone who was white or black could ever understand my Korean identity. I had a different way of knowing and understanding the world, due to my Korean heritage. Equally problematic was that my white teachers could not make the classroom experience culturally relevant for me (e.g. Gay, 2010; Ladson-Billings, 2000; Turner, 2003), since I was the only Korean student in the entire school. I was the only visible minority who could not understand the English language. There were other visible minorities (e.g. African-Americans and Latinos/as) in the class, but they, at least, had access to linguistic capital. I quickly experienced this new context as a strange place, full of unfamiliar faces that spoke an incomprehensible language. Although my first mission was to master the English language, other issues surfaced – my African-American and white classmates called me 'chink', and told me to go back to my country. Ironically, the name-calling and unfriendly faces somehow made me stronger. It motivated me more to continue learning in US classrooms, although I felt that no one could understand what it was like to be in my shoes. I think the names I was called have somehow been a part of my struggle to truly identify myself as a non-native English speaker (NNES), and to embrace a self-concept characterized by cultural and linguistic multiplicity (e.g. Braine, 1999; Kamhi-Stein, 2004).

Autobiographical Poetic Wave Two: Legitimization of Hyphenated Identities in Higher Education

A garden full of beautiful chrysanthemums
Different colors and heights
Often feeling privileged for being different,
Speaking English as an additional language,
Embracing diversity and significant milestone
Being championed for my bilingual-ness

> Another garden full of red roses
> As red as the loss of love
> *Ridiculed for accented English*
> *Perceived as an illegitimate English teacher*
> *Seen as an inferior and lesser gender*
> *Without a PhD in hand*

With a psychology degree, I found my first full-time job as an educational intern in a private K–12 school in the US. My role was to bring visibility and multicultural awareness to a predominantly white institution as an intern in Grades 1–3. The thought that one non-white person could change the racial climate of a predominantly white school was absurd, but I was excited about working with students.

Although I realized that teaching in general, specifically a lower grade level, was not part of my undergraduate training, I wanted to teach, to remain in an educational setting. In 1995, after living and being schooled in the US for 20-something years, I returned to my native country, Korea. Through relatives in Korea, I found a job as an educational consultant and a program developer in one of the foreign language institutes in the heart of Korea. The problem was that I did not have any background in English language teaching, nor did I know how to develop and create a curriculum for English learners, but my bilingual and bicultural identities secured the job for me. I acted as a cultural and linguistic broker between the director of the institute and the native English teachers – the most difficult job ever! My first year in Korea opened my eyes to culturally challenging situations. It was difficult for Koreans to appreciate that my upbringing for the past several decades in the US had already shaped my identities to some degree. Even more puzzling to them was that I spoke Korean fluently, just like them.

As far as the teaching was concerned, I had an opportunity to teach a diverse group of students: Teaching K–12 Korean students as well as teachers of K–12 Korean students in Korea. These K–12 teachers in Korea were struggling to meet the new English curriculum requirements handed down from the Department of Education in 1997 (Goto-Butler, 2004, 2007; Nunan, 2003). After two years of working as an EAL/English as an international language (EIL) teacher and administrator, I left the language institute to work in a university just outside Seoul in 1998. I needed this change in the TESOL industry, because I saw language institutes in Korea as money-making business enterprises that failed to take into consideration the diverse needs of EAL students (Reuckers & Ivers, 2015). I realized later that the university was not that much different from language institutes in South Korea.

Although I was thrilled to land a position in a university, I felt discriminated against due to issues involving my gender, my ethnicity and my linguistic abilities when interacting with Korean professors at times.

I felt that I was not taken seriously by the Korean professors when I shared my ideas about how to make the English language program better. In addition to my 'inferior' gender, which meant that I was not taken seriously when making decisions, there was an invisible power struggle between the Koreans and the Korean-Americans. Korean-Americans were not seen as 'real' Koreans, since they had abandoned their heritage to 'assimilate' or become socialized into American cultural practices. I have never imagined that I would be marginalized by my 'own kind', just as Xia was further disenfranchised by a Chinese immigrant woman at her university's part-time assessment program (Lee & Simon-Maeda, 2006; Park, 2012). Furthermore, Korean professors perceived my highly proficient English language ability as a threat rather than as a resource. I realized that my racial identity positioned me as a Korean English professor, but my fluency in English, compared to the Korean professors and my teacher identities were far removed from traditional approaches. Disenchanted by the societal-level discourses that further marginalized my identity as a bilingual, Korean, transnational and US-educated English teacher in Korea, I returned to the US in July 1998. I wanted to expand my professional credentials by earning master's and doctoral degrees in TESOL. I felt ridiculed in my home country just because I had immigrated to the US at an early age, had become fluent in an additional language, and received little understanding of what my lived experiences must have been for the past few decades.

These higher education degrees in the TESOL field, such as an MA and PhD, would provide me with more legitimacy as a university English instructor in Korea, so I thought. I applied to an MATESOL program in the US, and began my studies in January 1999 at a university in the northeast part of the US.

Autobiographical Poetic Wave Three: Epistemological and Ontological Revolution

A garden full of beautiful chrysanthemums
Different colors and heights
Knowledge constructed around
Race, class, gender and language
Privileging identities as an Immigrant NNES
Affect what, how and why I research

Another garden full of red roses
As red as the loss of love
Politics around conducting research
Disenfranchised by immigrant NNES-ness
Language intersects race, gender, class
Affect what, how and why I research

In my MATESOL program, I was the only 'hyphenated' NNES, in the sense that I was the only migrant NNES while the rest of my NNES colleagues were international students. Now I understand that these constructs (migrant and international) are problematic, since they do not illustrate the level of fluidity within and across individuals, but those were the labels used. Although my international NNES colleagues saw me as a resource, I felt alone as the only hyphenated individual. Because my experiences were so different from theirs, it was difficult for me to claim an insider positionality vis-à-vis my international colleagues. I'm sure that the experiences of my international NNES colleagues were also diverse. Even with these perceived challenges, I successfully completed my MATESOL program and started my PhD program in TESOL in order to commence work as an educational researcher.

I entered the field of educational research in 2000. In one of my first graduate seminar classes in the doctoral program, 'Theory and Research on Teaching', I came to understand and accept the ever-present conundrum that conducting educational research is political. I also came to understand that the capitalist system seldom works justly for *all* people. Upon that realization, coupled with the initial questions emerging from my interactions with colleagues from diverse linguistic and racial contexts, I chose to focus my research on the themes of race, class, gender and language teacher identity in TESOL programs. This focus highlights my commitment to researching the lives and experiences of East Asian women teachers (as well as other visible minority teachers) of English in US TESOL programs. Specifically, I continued to focus on how an English teacher's perceived linguistic identity impacts her teacher identity, and how English teachers' self-marginalized racial and linguistic identities coexist with their privileged class and academic identities. A series of published articles has demonstrated my commitment to continue to focus on how women teachers of English from all over the world (specifically, the Middle East, Africa and East Asia) experience their US TESOL programs. My research has evolved into seeking out my ever-changing identities, and those of women similar to myself, in the context of our multilingual backgrounds, values and beliefs in schooling and pedagogy, and our lived experiences as multilinguals, for they 'affect what, how, and why I research (Ladson-Billings, 2000: 268).

Autobiographic Poetic Wave Four: Perception of Mama PhDs

> A garden full of beautiful chrysanthemums
> Different colors and heights
> *Embracing my competing identities:*
> *Teacher-Scholar, Mom, Spouse*

> Another garden full of red roses
> As red as the loss of love
> *Societal level discourses places*
> *Mama PhDs as*
> *Less productive and less competitive*

Finding the courage to explore, voice, and advocate

This line of critical research inquiry has sustained me for many years, though upon completing my PhD in 2006, my competing identity as a newly married woman in her late thirties started to take precedence: Staying pregnant was the most difficult task I had ever embarked on in my life. My husband and I had given up on having a child of our own, and were preparing documents for an international adoption, so we sought the assistance of the Catholic Charities of Baltimore. Around the same time, I was asked to teach not only sections of advanced, pre-academic English language courses at the community college, but also a couple of sections of in-service teachers at the state university as well. Although I was seeking a tenure-track position upon completing my PhD, my difficult pregnancy, coupled with being a married woman, limited our mobility as a couple. In August 2007, I was pregnant for the third time. By the time I was 15 weeks into my pregnancy, I was fully immersed in teaching two courses at the community college and two courses in the teacher education program. I also had three successful on-campus interviews for a tenure-track position while seven months pregnant.

In August 2008, I began my tenure-track position at my current institution as a new mom of a three-month-old child. Although nothing was directly stated to me about my identity as a new mom, I sensed it. I felt it. I lived it. A perceived social stigma associated with being a newly minted mom in a world of academia often pushed me to do more than I was asked to do, and these issues appropriately surfaced in my teaching and scholarship inquiry. According to Evans and Grant (2008), many mama PhDs experienced (self-perceived) marginalization around their abilities as teachers and scholars in the academy. There was an expectation that moms in the university would be less productive and more problematic in terms of teaching and scholarly activities (Castaneda & Isgro, 2013). In my own case, I sensed that I was offered below my well-deserved salary rank due to societal-level discourses that often place women with children on the margin. We are often seen as less productive and less competitive. Perhaps this perceived attitude unconsciously made me resist further negotiating with the administrators on my deserved salary rank. At the same time, I believe this perceived attitude and discourses around what mama PhDs could or could not do pushed me more than usual to do my best in my teacher scholarship. Ironically, although there was an element of self-perceived marginalization as a result of my assigned and embraced identity, I was also comfortable being at my institution, where I was able to do the type of work I was prepared to do. My consistency in teaching and scholarly productivity surprised my colleagues, yet I was doing what I had set out to do as an assistant professor in a tenure-track position. According to Hanauer (2012: 5), 'personal insight' focuses on 'integrating a reflective process that leads to a deepened appreciation and understanding of personal experience (and, ultimately, greater understanding of the human condition)'. My identity as a new mom in a tenure-track position had allowed me to shine, manage my time and be just as or more productive than my peers in my programs.

While I was being productive at school, my son thrived at the university day care. Although I often felt unscrupulous for leaving him at the day care for long days, he seemed to do well. Due to my guilty conscience, I capitalized on the hours I had at school so that I could give Aidan 100% of my time at home. In the first couple of years, I often came in at eight in the morning and focused on my teaching and research until five in the afternoon, when I left to pick up my son. On days when my husband picked him up, I stayed later at school to get more work done. Even on the days when I did not teach, I came to school and locked myself in my office, which was about five-by-seven-feet in size with no sunlight. From 2008 to 2012, just before I went up for tenure and promotion in fall 2012, I had published six single-authored refereed journal articles, one co-edited book, one book chapter and three co-authored refereed journal articles, and I had six refereed journal articles in preparation bearing the name of my institution. In terms of teaching, I taught across the programs represented in my department: 12 undergraduate classes and 14 graduate classes in total. I consistently received high evaluations on areas that mattered for students and their learning. I share these details to illustrate the profound effect that my identity as a new mom in academia, coupled with my lived experiences, has had on my work in higher education thus far, and what this may mean for being and becoming mothers in the academy.

Han Nah has shown me so much about what it means to wrestle with motherhood in academia. As I am writing this book, I am constantly reminded of her wisdom in gently nudging me to give myself breathing room as a married woman with a child when it comes to academic work. I am forever grateful to Han Nah and other academic mothers for sharing those words of wisdom as one way to understand who I am now and what I can do in the years to come as a mama scholar, woman in the academy, writer and teacher educator.

Notes

(1) With the *L2 Journal*'s permission, the beginning of this chapter comes from Park (2013a).
(2) I have been collecting autobiographical writings since early 2000, when I commenced my doctoral work at University of Maryland, College Park. These autobiographical writings were completed between 2000 and 2006 as part of course assignments, research projects in collaboration with faculty and other doctoral students, and portions of teaching materials at the community college. My additional data are the *Untitled*, written in 1984, as well as the extended versions of this poem, written while writing this chapter between July 2012 and May 2013.
(3) This is a poem I wrote in 1984 as part of a course assignment.
(4) The Roman text is from the original *Untitled* poem written in 1984, while the italic text is what was added when writing this chapter in 2012/2013.

2 Exposing our Discourses of Privilege and Marginalization: Gender, Race and Class Connections to Teaching English[1]

> ... [C]reating safe spaces for teacher candidates to wrestle with issues of race, class, gender, ..., to reflect upon intersectionality, and to consider how marginalization and privilege can occur simultaneously within the classroom community and broader sociohistorical and political spaces. Such work can help teacher educators unpack how English can be a symbol of power and privilege and yet serve a marginalizing function ...
> Varghese et al., 2016: 20

I begin this chapter with the epigraph excerpted from *TESOL Quarterly*'s 2016 Special Issue 'Language Teacher Identities in (Multi)lingual Educational Contexts' as one way to highlight the critical nature of the race–gender–social class connection to the teaching of English in our lives as women. The women and I revealed our intimate stories that have been deeply buried in our hearts and minds, which have cut across issues of race, gender and class. All of these constructs working together often leads to understanding how privilege and marginalization coexist as they relate to issues of power, privilege and (il)legitimacy of English language (EL). Moreover, this is how these constructs are normalized in a broader society, where certain ideologies, behaviors, individuals and discourses are encouraged and celebrated (Kubota, 2004; Motha, 2014; Park, 2015).

I can confidently state that English has always had an overpowering and (il)legitimate presence in our lives. Through a multitude of opportunities – immigration, English education policy, personal and professional endeavors – each one of us interacted with English in more ways than one. The language that is supposed to provide us with expanded opportunities in a new land (and for most of us, it provided us with renewing opportunities in our home countries) has often moved us into a space of silence and marginalization. English as a symbolic capital has turned into a source of symbolic violence (Bourdieu, 1991; Lin, 1999). Without truly understanding the politics around the EL, we wanted to be pedagogues who would awe and empower our students and, at the same time, legitimize our linguistic and teacher identities (Clarke, 2008; Ha, 2008; Varghese et al., 2005, 2016). In many ways, through writing this book, we begin to unfold the politics around who we are as teachers of English to speakers of other languages (TESOL), East Asian women teachers of English and daughters/spouses/mothers in academia (Castaneda & Isgro, 2013; Park, 2013; Varghese et al., 2016).

Throughout my research inquiry and in the process of writing this book, a sense of comradeship and intimacy grew, as we encouraged each other to share the collective stories that have always been a part of our identity construction. We came to realize that our privileges were often masked by all the marginalizing issues we experienced (Park, 2015; Park et al., 2016; Vandrick, 2009, 2011, 2014). According to James (2007: 167), 'gaining perspective outside [and inside] of our own experience and thinking about the consequences of our being for ourselves and others' can become a foundation for promoting caring pedagogies, which is also echoed in the work of Sonia Nieto (2010) and Nel Noddings (1987, 1988). For example, as an emerging English language teacher (ELT) specialist journeying through a doctoral program in a prestigious research institution, I never even thought about my own privilege of navigating through a terminal degree program in the US. I only focused on being different and feeling different from my nonnative English-speaking ([N]NES) colleagues in my program, while those very (N)NES colleagues often perceived me as a capable doctoral colleague. Specifically, I was often in awe of my colleagues' perceived white privilege, without reflecting on my own privilege as a woman from an East Asian context in higher education. Being white and sounding like a native speaker were important characteristics during those days: I know! How ludicrous! What was I thinking? (Motha, 2014; Varghese et al., 2016). More often than not, I felt like I was sinking in a pool of issues related to not being able to own my academic writing and navigating the discourses pervasive in my academic field. I have always felt like an outsider, ever since I stepped into this country with my parents in 1976. Even as I pen this book, I am feeling vulnerable due to my perceived identity as an (il)legitimate and peripheral member in the world of publishing in academia, and my (un)welcomed strategies in navigating the geopolitics of academic publishing (Canagarajah, 2002; Lillis & Curry, 2010). On the other hand, the fact that I am actually compiling a book as a tenured faculty in a US higher education institution is a product of my privileged status.

This privileged status often goes unnoticed and under-researched due to the compounding affect that marginalization might have on our lives (Park, 2015; Park et al., 2016; Vandrick, 2009, 2011, 2014). However, the EL, while being a definite resource for those who use the language to communicate, can also be a marginalizing force for many around the globe. This co-existence of privilege and marginalization in one's experience is under-researched in TESOL in general, and in the experiences of EL professionals from diverse contexts in particular. In this book, I hope to uncover the co-existence of privilege and marginalization in the lives of six women teachers of English from diverse East Asian contexts. To this end, this chapter is a rendition of how I come to understand the literature on critical perspectives on teaching English and how the literature, coupled with my lived experiences, has served my understanding of the gender–race–class connections to teaching English. Therefore, I move away from repeating what has already been widely published in the field, and briefly focus on how I come to understand and own the race–gender–class connection to teaching English for the women in the book.

Understanding our Gendered Identity as Social and Discursive Construction

In my decision to foreground our narratives focused on the critical and feminist perspectives, I embrace the progressive paradigm and post-structuralist turn (Aneja, 2016; Motha, 2014; Weedon, 1987) of understanding women's identities as multiple, fluid, contradictory and socially/discursively constructed. From these perspectives, I am compelled to find ways to address the lives and experiences of women living inside and outside multiple linguistic, cultural and sociopolitical contexts, and at the same time, interrogate my own privileges (Davis & Skilton-Sylvester, 2004; Ha, 2008; Higgins, 2010; Menard-Warwick, 2004, 2005, 2009; Motha, 2014; Pavlenko, 2004; Pavlenko & Blackledge, 2004; Pavlenko et al., 2001; Vandrick, 2009; Vitanova, 2004). Even within certain sociocultural and sociopolitical contexts, there is a continuous shaping and contention of gendered identities (Simon-Maeda, 2004). As women from diverse East Asian contexts living in the US, navigating both the patriarchal and democratic systems, we were often conflicted about our perceived, and often multiple and conflicting, gender roles. As I pen this book, I am once again reminded of Han Nah's reflection on living with the multiple and complex experiences that have shaped her identities:

> I think if I were a man, I would not get this kind of very complex experience. Because I am a woman, I had to stop many things due to my circumstance [a daughter, spouse, mother]. I could not keep continuing to pursue my educational or professional path. (Han Nah, interview, April 19)

Similarly, there have been many discussions about how teaching is a gendered profession, because women are often seen as more nurturing and caring (e.g. Maher & Ward, 2002; Noddings, 1988). Just as the female gender has been explored and researched as subjugated 'subjects' in the literature, the male gender has been privileged in the scholarly venue, often as subjugators.

As such, in second language acquisition and applied linguistics, much research – and in TESOL, much theorizing – has been done and recited by white, male scholars; the voices of women scholars, especially the voices of women of color, have been scarce (Lin *et al.*, 2004; Norton & Pavlenko, 2004; Pennycook, 1999). To this end, proponents of feminist perspectives, whether they are advocating for African-American women, Latina women, Asian-American women or other women of color, 'applied their tools to building knowledge of women's oppression and, based on that knowledge, to developing strategies for resisting subordination and improving women's lives' (McCann & Kim, 2003: 1).

With this understanding of how the issues of gender are fused into language learning and language teacher education, there has been a plethora of studies examining various issues of gender in relation to language teaching and language teacher education (Amin, 1997, 2001; Davis & Skilton-Sylvester, 2004; Higgins, 2010; Langman, 2004; Menard-Warwick, 2004, 2005; Morita, 2004; Motha, 2004; Park, 2006; Simon-Maeda, 2004; Skapoulli, 2004; Vitanova, 2004; Warriner, 2004). Among those studies examining gender as a discursive and social construction, very few studies focus on how women of color, 'visible minority women' (Amin, 2001), or NNES women from East Asian countries, such as Han Nah, navigate the multiple gender identities imposed on them by their sociocultural, sociopolitical and familial contexts.

Further complicating our gendered identity, our motherhood (for Han Nah and myself) became both a source of privilege and of marginalization, as some of us traversed different professional spaces (e.g. Baxley, 2012; Brown *et al.*, 2002; Castaneda & Isgro, 2013; Evans & Grant, 2008; Gordon & Keyfitz, 2004; Johnson-Bailey, 2015; Lin, 2004; Norton & Toohey, 2004; O'Laughlin & Bischoff, 2005; Valian, 2005; Anders, 2004; van den Brink & Benschop, 2012). As Han Nah has clearly depicted for me in the following excerpt, I witnessed how 'my identity as an Asian woman [soon to be married] seemed to be implicated in her reflective process in relation to her own experience [as a married woman]' (Lee & Simon-Maeda, 2006: 582):

> You may feel that after you get married, you may not be successful that much in your studies. After you get married, you never compare with someone who never gets married and just study. You can find a woman who can work for you. [Your] mother [can] take care of your child, and your housework; then you can work outside and you can maybe work inside and outside. (Han Nah, interview, 15 February)

Sensing the Racialized and Classed Discourses in our English-Language Teaching Identities

The gender construct is not the only identity marker that influenced our transnational process of being and becoming ELTs. Motha (2014: 26) reminds me that examining these discourses [gender, race, class, etc.] individually does not 'indicate in any way that they are separable, not to represent [ELT] in any symbolic way. Rather, they are examined individually to demonstrate clearly the relevance of each within a matrix of complicated relationships.)' Being visible minority women in the field of TESOL, we have continued to perceive ourselves to be less than our NES colleagues, in that we have needed to work harder than native English speakers (NESs) to claim our credibility and legitimacy as ELTs. It is important to raise awareness of how powerfully race, specifically the white race, is equated with legitimacy, power, credibility and being 'better' in relation to teaching English (e.g. Amin, 2001; Faez, 2011; Frankenberg, 2001; Ha, 2008; Kubota & Lin, 2006; Motha, 2014; Park, 2015; Tang, 1997). These powerful, often debilitating discourses, absent in our native educational spaces, became part of our lived experiences in the US. Motha (2014: 37) discusses the 'invisibility of racism in ELT ...' in that 'Racism has become so naturalized within the project of teaching English that its presence is no longer noticeable'. Many English teaching job advertisements still require English teachers to be white, native speakers only (Reucker & Ives, 2015; Yoon, 2014). What is even more incapacitating is equating fluent English communicative abilities and EL teaching identity with privileged class status. In that, there is also a sense of urgency that comes with teaching English in such status-conscious societies as Korea, China, Taiwan and Japan. Due to the increase in globalization and internationalization influencing educational policy, economic mobility and international collaboration, the TESOL market continues to explode to the point of hiring locally prepared teachers and US-educated teachers with certain qualities important in teaching English: white, female, native speaker of English, standard American English accent (Ruecker & Ives, 2015; Yoon, 2014). Challenging these unrealistic goals of native-speakerism ideology in the TESOL market is our foremost advocacy work toward dismantling the issues of power and privilege inherent in the TESOL industry.

Furthermore, it is crucial to unpack the types of capital that have been bestowed on us to be part of TESOL programs in English-speaking countries. In particular, how types of capital have been 'erased' due to the increased emphasis on issues of marginalization needs scholarly attention. This 'erasure' identity is often masked by discursively constructed notions of what it means to be marginalized due to English teachers' linguistic and racial identities (Park, 2015). For instance, Ibrahim (2008), Motha (2006, 2014) and Kubota and Lin (2006) argue that it is important to directly confront race and racism in the TESOL profession, instead of continuously 'operating under erasure' (Ibrahim, 2008: 56). Similarly, many teacher education students who come from all over the world come with a lot of privilege, and while many assume that linguistic and racial marginalization trump the types of capital they may possess, the TESOL field needs to be more critically conscious about eradicating the possible 'erasure' of competing discourses of privilege (Ibrahim, 2008; MacDonald, 2007; Shuck, 2006). In other words, how do issues of privilege (forms of capital) coexist with issues of marginalization in the lives of language users? While much work has been done to explore the issues of gender, race and ethnicity in relation to language learning and teaching, the construct of social class has been scarce in looking at the learners and teachers (Kanno, 2014; Vandrick, 2014). Hence, research on groups of learners coming from more privileged settings, such as East Asian women matriculated into US TESOL programs, has remained scarce. The notion that education is a fundamental human right, and not a privilege (Price, 2002) needs to be revisited for our journeys. For many of us, educational attainment, especially in the US, was a product of our privileged status (while many of us are on different points of the privilege spectrum), which gave us an edge in terms of educational pursuits to the point of immigrating to the US or being admitted into US TESOL programs.

Due to our privileged backgrounds, we gained different forms of capital, involving learning and teaching English and gaining admission into TESOL programs. Additionally, most of us came with economic resources that would sustain us until the completion of our degree programs. All six of us, some more than others, came to an English-speaking country with a set of beliefs and knowledge, identities and dispositions characterized by this privilege. However, these forms of capital became nullified or devalued in the US TESOL programs (Messekher, 2012; Park et al., 2016). In other words, fields (spaces in which our identities are (de)/(re)constructed) are mutable, depending on what forms of capital are valued in those particular contexts (Bourdieu, 1977; Gao, 2014; Kanno, 2014; Park, 2015; Park et al., 2016; Shin, 2014; Vandrick, 2014). For those claiming nonnative English-speaking teacher (NNEST) identity, like these women and myself, experiencing (self-perceived) marginalization may have occurred as a result of possible normative attitudes and behaviors around the global presence of the EL, equated with 'American' and 'whiteness' identities (Motha, 2014). For instance, a (self) marginalization process can occur due to: (1) one's native language being other than English; (2) how the EL is situated in local and global contexts; (3) one's visible minority race; and (4) lack of access to linguistic, cultural and social capital that could provide a person with certain symbolic capital in the future, as well as the complex interconnectedness of these identity constructs (e.g. Amin, 2001; Braine, 2005; Davis & Skilton-Sylvester, 2004; Kamhi-Stein, 2004a, 2004b; Kanno, 2014; Kubota & Lin, 2006; Kumashiro, 2000, 2002; Lee, 2006, 2009; Park, 2008, 2009, 2012; Sharkey & Johnson, 2003; Shuck, 2006; Tang, 1997; Vandrick, 2009, 2014; Varghese *et al.*, 2005, 2016).

As documented by scholars, these marginalized experiences may come about as a result of reproducing the dominant ideology pervasive in the worldwide TESOL enterprise, which privileges and places more credibility and legitimacy, whether knowingly or unknowingly, on white NESTs, and sometimes on white NNESTs as well (e.g. Amin, 2001; Kubota & Lin, 2006; Kumaravadivelu, 2003; Lin *et al.*, 2002). In other words, there is a need to disrupt the normative discourses and repetition of certain discourses, knowledges and practices that are pervasive in TESOL. Within these normative discourses, the NNESTs begin to compare themselves to NESTs, realizing that 'language and race are closely linked as a means of distinguishing Self and Other' (Shrake, 2006: 259). This close connection was depicted in Motha's (2006, 2014) work. Motha (2006: 504) discussed the racial identity dilemma of one of her participants, Katie, a Korean-born woman, who '… sensed that her [Katie's] authority was in question because of her racial identity, and she was influenced by her own history of shame about her race'.

The racial privilege prevalent in the lives of white NESTs may become crucial in understanding the intersection of privilege and marginalization and the extent to which privilege for one group may contribute to marginalization for another (i.e. Kumashiro, 2000; Kubota & Lin, 2006; Reucker & Ives, 2015; Shuck, 2006). For instance, Kubota and Lin (2006) argue that 'white privilege' is the normative yet invisible nature of whiteness observed in everyday practices and discourse. It has been argued that whiteness exerts its power as an invisible and unmarked norm against which all Others are racially and culturally defined, marked and made inferior (Kubota & Lin, 2006: 483). The identity of 'the normative yet invisible nature of whiteness' challenges NNESTs' racial and linguistic identities as EL users and teachers, further contributing to feelings of marginalization. This type of power exertion can also be seen in white NNESTs, as was illustrated in the work of Kubota and McKay (2009: 601), which depicted Brazilians who look like Americans (meaning white Brazilians), as opposed to dark-skinned Brazilians, working and living in rural Japan.

Just as it is important to understand the extent to which privilege for one group may contribute to marginalization for another, it is equally important to discern the extent to which privilege intersects with marginalization for a certain group of individuals as a way to understand how different forms of capital play out in individuals' journeys (Park, 2015). Many international undergraduate and graduate students enrolled in US universities can be identified as having varying forms of privilege, and have been called students of new global elites (SONGEs) (Vandrick, 1995, 2011, 2014). This assigned identity stems from the fact that studying abroad in English-speaking countries does require much in the way of economic, educational and social capital in terms of viewing educational opportunities and values attached to education in US contexts (e.g. Bourdieu, 1986; Grimshaw & Sears, 2008; Shin, 2014; Song, 2009; Vandrick, 1995).

Most come through sponsorship from their government, schools and family. However, for almost all of them, transcultural educational opportunities would be nonexistent if economic support were not available, since it would take at least two years (more for doctoral programs) to complete a master's program in the field of TESOL, and there are very few scholarship and fellowship opportunities available for MA-level students. Both Liu and Xia were provided with assistantships at Pacific University; however, they still needed additional income to pay for their living expenses. In other words, these women came with a lot of cultural, social and economic capital, which placed them on the continuum of having ample privilege to be immersed in the US educational contexts. However, in the published literature, much of the work that examines the lives and experiences of NNES professionals focuses on the ways in which these individuals have experienced marginalization due to their perceived distance from the TESOL profession and their nonnativeness, without emphasizing the privileged endowed to them/us. In other words, their privileged identities are often erased. More importantly, all of us were focused on the value of US TESOL program education without questioning the disconnectedness of the US-based curricula and pedagogies to the very educational philosophies in our native countries (Bhattacharya, 2011; Kubota, 2004; Park, 2012).

While Pierre Bourdieu's work has been theorized by studying the lives of Algerian peasants, his discussion of the types of capital that individuals may possess can shed some light on my work. Bourdieu (1986) and Bourdieu and Passeron (1977) challenged the notion that one's social class has the possibility of transforming the cultural resources to which individuals have access in their environment. As for the women in the study, their upper-middle to upper-class status in their native countries gave them opportunities to learn other languages, study and live in foreign countries and, ultimately, gain admission into TESOL programs in the US. Moreover, Bourdieu argued that different experiences in an individual's home life could facilitate and expand a person's academic achievement. For the women in the study, the 'different experiences' were opportunities of language enrichment programs in their native countries, living and learning in other countries and, ultimately, earning a degree in the US. Grounded in the Bourdieusian framework, Park *et al.* (2016) documented a study focusing on two undergraduate West African students matriculated in a US undergraduate teacher education program. The authors found that, for the two teacher candidates, context-specific capital emerged from power equated to access. Similarly, Grant and Wong (2008: 176, cited in Park *et al.*, 2016: 9) argued that 'such capital is not simply something one has, but something that has different value in different contexts, mediated by relation of power and knowledge in different social fields'. As such, a degree from the US was a form of symbolic capital that could potentially transform their lived experiences into something more meaningful and worthwhile as they imagined their future identities and possibilities. Similarly, Messekher's (2012) research findings on the Algerian graduate students in the US were consistent with forms of capital being devalued across multiple spaces. As such, it can be argued that forms of capital are not static, given teachers' transnational mobility. In fact, these forms of capital can be in competition, depending on the participants, their goals and educational history, just to name a few factors.

Moreover, Bourdieu and Passeron (1977) suggested that being part of a high social-class status with abundant cultural resources was connected to educational success. In all of their cases, either their parents or the spouses (for those who were married) worked toward providing them with various forms of capital as a means toward their educational success. In other words, their family members provided resources (i.e. cultural capital, symbolic capital and other forms of capital), which yielded important social, cultural and educational profits in the cases of the five women. While differing in age groups with the women in my study, Shin (2014: 100) discussed 'early study abroad' (ESA), a form of transnational educational migration that Korean families embark on for their young children (usually children who are in K–12), also known as 'geroge gajok (wild geese family)'. The following is what Shin argued about ESA:

> ESA represents a Korean middle-class's strategy to reproduce social position by creating new capital of distinction (Bourdieu, 1984) in response to the increasingly intense competition in the Korean job market and education, which has been growing since the 1990s. (Shin, 2014: 100)

Similarly, Song's (2010: 23) interview findings with Korean ESA families in the US state that 'their attitudes to language education were closely related to the language ideologies of global English in Korea. That is, these early study abroad families circulated "*glo*calized" English (localized global English) through transnational migration as an educational strategy'. In other words, countries such as South Korea, if equipped with economic resources and forms of capital to support those resources, are pouring their resources into educational migration to access 'authentic' English and US academic degrees in an effort to become more marketable in the global economy, a form of 'linguistic instrumentalism' in a neoliberal society at work (Kubota, 2011: 248). According to Kubota (2011: 248), linguistic instrumentalism is intimately connected to human capital, since individuals need to continue to access linguistic and global skills in order to compete in the global market to reach certain levels of economic viability. For Han Nah, Liu, Xia, Yu Ri and Shu-Ming (to varying degrees), their immigration, their short-term language learning programs, their professional contacts with NESs in their home countries and their admission into US TESOL programs become part of their journeys of linguistic instrumentalism. Their educational journeys hone in on being competitive in the worldwide contexts and being symbolic representatives from their home countries.

Both Han Nah and Yu Ri had experienced ESA (different time periods: Han Nah in high school and college; Yu Ri in middle school), which had an impact on their decision to become TESOL professionals. As for Liu and Xia, their interactions in English during their elementary school years occurred with NESTs working in China. Whether most of the EL learning occurred in the public schools or private language classes, the women had access to learning English beginning in their elementary school years. Although some could argue that all grade-school students in these East Asian countries had access to learning English, due to mandates from the ministries of education in these countries, the five women had special connections with English. This culminated in the realization of unique experiences for them, commensurate with their privileged-class status. In addition to what they gained from their EL learning communities in their native countries, they were given opportunities to go abroad to live and learn in foreign countries or to teach English (as was the case with Shu-Ming). Without the resources from their privileged backgrounds, the women would not have been able to partake of these cultural, linguistic and professional experiences. Their short-term study abroad language learning and/or teaching experiences in Germany (Xia's degree program), Turkey (Han Nah's degree and language learning programs), US (Han Nah and Yu Ri's degree and language learning programs), England (Han Nah's language learning program) and Taiwan (Shu-Ming's teaching experience) afforded them cultural and linguistic capital, which, coupled with other resources, enabled them to begin TESOL degree programs in the US. Although each woman had different reasons for choosing to matriculate into TESOL programs in the US, their experiences in navigating various foreign cultures and languages gave them the additional investment to begin these TESOL programs. Despite having come to this country with varying forms of privilege, enabling them to attend degree programs abroad, NNESTs continue to remain largely invisible in the literature with respect to research on the intersection of privilege and marginalization in the shaping of their identities.

One possible interpretation for the lack of discourses pertaining to the intersection of privilege and marginalization for NNESTs, specifically for Asians and Asian Americans, despite their visibility in the US degree programs, may be due to how Asians and Asian Americans have been perceived of as a 'model minority' and/or 'honorary whites' (e.g. Lee, 2005, 2009; Lee & Kumashiro, 2005; Ngo & Lee, 2007; Tuan, 2003). The construction of 'model minority' emerged in the 1960s with a success story of Japanese Americans in the *New York Times* essay (Lee, 2009). This construction historically placed different peoples of Asian descent into a single grouping of Asians or Asian Americans, and much scholarship problematizes the model minority construct since it places all Asians and Asian Americans into a group of 'studious' individuals (e.g. Lee, 2006; Ngo & Lee, 2007; Pang, 2006). This mythical depiction further places individuals from Asian descent against African Americans, since the term 'model minority' assumes that there is a group of minorities that are less than perfect. Lee (2009) views the stereotype of 'model minority' as exemplifying the 'achievement ideology' by indirectly stating the following:

> African-Americans should model themselves after Asian Americans. While Asian Americans were held up as shining examples of hard work and good citizenship, African Americans were positioned as loud, complaining, and lazy. As a hegemonic device, the model minority stereotype maintains the dominance of whites in the racial hierarchy by diverting attention away from racial inequalities and by setting standings for how minorities should behave. (Lee, 2009: 7)

Similarly, Ngo and Lee (2007: 416) argue that 'the model minority stereotype is used to silence and contain Asian Americans even as it silences other racial groups ...'. Furthermore, Lee (2006: 17) claims that the 'categorization of [model minority] itself implies a kind of homogeneity ...', which may not take into consideration the hybrid identities among Asians:

> [The model minority construction] erases significant differences related to ethnicity, social class, language, generation, history, gender, sexual orientation, disability, religion, immigration status, and region. It obscures the fact that some students are not doing well in school. ... This stereotype also diverts attention away from the racial inequities faced by Asians, and it suggests that they have overcome racial barriers to achieve success. (Lee & Kumarshiro, 2005: xi–xii)

Added to this racialized discursive construction is the notion of social class and how class identities become further exploited as well as silenced. Interconnected with the 'model minority' normative discourse is how society, as a whole, suppresses conversations about economic class, even though it is crucial in understanding the state of perpetual marginalization of certain groups of individuals, due to their relegation as 'have-nots' or even as 'haves' (Adams *et al.*, 2010). Vandrick (1995: 376) states, 'in the US we tend not to want to talk about class, feeling that our society, at least, aims to be a classless society, where everyone has equal opportunity to succeed'. This 'erasure' type of discourse, focusing on social class, has been pervasive, and it is important to unpack and problematize this type of discursive construction. Vandrick (2014) further argues:

> Social class status can cause great disadvantage or grant great privilege. Because it has such concrete consequences, it is important that those involved in language education, whether teaching language, preparing language educators, or carrying out research on language education, consider addressing social class in their teaching and research. (Vandrick, 2014: 90)

In other words, it is important to be mindful of how issues of privilege coexist with marginalization in our lives. As such, TESOL professionals need to directly confront such discourses, especially in language (teacher) education.

Along the same line, Lee (2006) discovered that middle-class, East Asian students were placed in the model minority category, and were often compared to middle-class white students in terms of achievement, which parallels 'achievement ideology', discussed earlier. Lee (2006) further denotes the additional complexities of the experiences of Asian Americans when looking specifically at social-class identity. Lee and other scholars exploring the experiences of Asian Americans (e.g. Ngo & Lee, 2007; Pang, 2006) state that a closer examination of the model minority as a group that achieved educational success reveals that this group is also economically successful. However, according to Lee (2006: 18), there is a significant gap between 'affluent Asian Americans who have achieved professional and/or entrepreneurial success and those who struggle to achieve marginal daily survival'. Moreover, she contends that the differences in educational achievement within the Asian American community may be related to differences in socioeconomic class, in that, '[e]thnic groups with high rates of poverty also experience low rates of educational attainment, and ethnic groups with low rates of poverty have higher levels of educational attainment' (Lee, 2006: 18).

Vandrick (2009: 6) acknowledges that 'academe itself is classed', describing ways in which 'for some socially privileged international/ESL students, including privileged women students, social class "trumped" gender … as most important and influential' (Vandrick, 2009: 88), perhaps mitigating some of the marginalization they may have experienced due to language and race as NNESTs. Hence, the 'model minority' construct and other images that essentialize a group of individuals need to be debunked in order to highlight the diversity in individuals from (East) Asian descent, and to accentuate the coexistence of privilege and marginalization in our lives.

Critiquing the Perceived Necessity and Desire to Earn an Academic Degree in the US

Many NNESTs interested in expanding their EL learning and teaching abilities desire to secure admission into US TESOL programs. Furthermore, many employers in their home countries look for employees with global awareness, global knowledge, English fluency and, in particular, those who have resided and have been educated in English-speaking countries, such as the US.

According to the Open Doors Report (2016)[2] published annually by the Institute of International Education, the number of international students in the US has increased 35.7% from 2010 to 2015 academic years:

- By 3% during the 2009–2010;
- By 4.7% during the 2010–2011;
- By 5.7% during the 2011–2012;
- By 7.2% during the 2012–2013;
- By 8.1% during the 2013–2014;
- By 10% during the 2014–2015

(Institute of International Education, 2016)

Although the Open Door Report does not specifically report the number of international students in TESOL degree programs, the report does indicate the number of international students in the US that matriculated in intensive English programs, and in the fields of education, foreign language and social sciences in which many US TESOL programs are housed. Published by the TESOL International Association, The English Language Professional's Resource Guide lists more than 400 TESOL programs in the US alone (MultiView, 2011). The sheer number of US programs likely heightens the visibility of the US as a place in which to pursue a TESOL degree. Moreover, the vast array of TESOL programs in the US reinforces the perception of the power and prestige of American Standard English (AmSE; see Bolton, 2005; McArthur, 2001; Phillipson, 1992). Challenging the very perception of power and prestige of AmSE, as well as problematizing Western-based pedagogies and/or US-based education (as well as from other Inner Circle countries [ICCs]), becomes critical in restructuring curricular approaches in TESOL programs.

The end of the 1990s was an important era for many countries in Kachru's (1997) Expanding Circle countries (ECCs) because of the spread of the EL with respect to issues of power and hegemony connected to the English language itself. This perception became a reality for these countries when their Ministry of Education mandated that curricular transformation, to include weekly mandatory English lessons with native speakers, become part of the educational policy (Goto-Butler, 2004, 2007; Nunan, 2003). While there is a need to critically examine how Kachru's concentric circles focus on the functions of the EL for those in these countries, it is important to note that Kachru's concentric circles of countries do not take into consideration transnationals – hybrid individuals who embrace more than one language and nationality.[3] With this continuous focus on globalization of EL learning and teaching, ICCs have continued to gain political and economic power over the Outer Circle countries (OCCs) and ECCs, even though the notion of World Englishes has slowly been overpowering the EL learning and teaching discourses around the world. As a result of this perception, many ELTs from OCCs and ECCs started to migrate to ICCs, not only to increase their EL proficiency, but also to become prepared to teach English around the world as a result of global mobility and the focus on internationalization (see Bolton, 2005; Jenkins, 2009; Kachru, 1997; Kamhi-Stein, 2000). Many from OCCs and ECCs seek admission into US TESOL programs to begin their academic and professional journeys as teachers of English (e.g. Bolton, 2005; Butler, 2007; Kamhi-Stein, 2000; Nunan, 2003). However, individuals originally from OCCs and ECCs, such as Han Nah, Liu, Xia, Yu Ri and Shu-Ming, may have had a lot of transnational experiences under their belts as a result of study abroad, immigration, etc. These complex transnational identities are often not taken into consideration in Kachru's paradigm.

Within the ECCs, people from countries such as Korea, China, Taiwan and Japan understood English to be their foreign language, a subject to be mastered and memorized in order to sound and act like NESs. As a result of this 'English fever' all over the ECCs, NESTs were a hot commodity to the point that English teachers were hired without sufficient professional or educational credentials as long as they were white and sounded like an NES with Standard English usage and an AmSE accent (e.g. Berns, 2005; Bolton, 2005; McArthur, 2001). In essence, individuals from ICCs and OCCs have more power to exercise their linguistic competence as well as their material resources over OCCs and ECCs in TESOL (Kachru, 1997; Oda, 1999). Again, Kachru's concentric circles in relation to the function of English are antiquated, since it is important to understand the movement of individuals in and out of countries around the world. This was certainly the case when I was teaching English in Korea in 1997, and it has continued to have a dominant, hegemonic impact in the ELT market around the world, especially in ECCs (Shin, 2014). Given this sociocultural and sociopolitical direction of the ELT industry, it is vital that TESOL programs around the globe, especially in the ICCs, raise critical consciousness around the power and privilege connected to the EL and its teaching. This kind of critical consciousness raising can only bring about 'meta-awareness' – that is, a 'heightened awareness of how their thinking evolves as they are being socialized into their disciplines', as 'you cannot, after all, address problems in your existing condition unless you have reflected on them and recognized your own participation in this condition' (Ramanathan, 2002: 2, cited in Motha, 2014: xxiii).

In order to understand the impact that the globalization of the EL has had on their educational policy and pedagogy, Nunan (2003) surveyed some of the ECCs. The results of Nunan's (2003: 606) findings indicated that '[t]eacher education and the EL skills of teachers in public-sector institutions are inadequate ... of even greater concern has to be the widespread use of nonqualified English teachers'. Instead of pouring economic resources into hiring NESTs from overseas, Nunan (2003: 608) argues that it would be beneficial 'to enhance the proficiency and professional skills of local teachers'. Supporting local teachers through EL training and boosting communication skills is also documented in Butler's (2004, 2007) study, which examined the proficiency levels of English as a foreign language (EFL) elementary-level teachers in China, Taiwan and Korea. Similarly, Liu et al. (2004) found that Korean English teachers would need to gradually increase the amount of EL that they used in classrooms, since most did not have the proficiency level to use English a great deal of the time. Liu et al.'s (2004: 633) study also indicates that in order for Korean teachers to use more EL in their teaching, 'curricula and assessment at both the national and local levels should be revised to focus on using language'. The challenges and limitations of curricula and assessment on the communicative competence of both teachers and students learning English in ECCs have been documented in other studies (e.g. Butler, 2004; Li, 1998; Kumaravadivelu, 2003; Nunan, 2003). Nunan did not specifically discuss the preparation of East Asian women teacher learners from ECCs in the ICCs. However, his collective case studies of EC (China, Taiwan, Korea and Japan) and OC (Malaysia and Hong Kong) countries did point out the need to better accommodate the professional and pedagogical needs of NNESTs receiving teacher preparation education in the ICCs, such as the US.

With the overpowering need to master the EL and have an 'American accent' as the most desirable level of fluency, in most Asian countries, students' sense of self is often related to how they did on college-entrance examinations, especially on the English component. The examination scores dictated the caliber of universities to which they were admitted, and the number of other accomplishments connected to the knowledge and fluency of English. The EL was simply a subject to be memorized and mastered; it was not considered a tool for communication in society. However, once the students were admitted into a university, with some opting to take English communication classes, they were dumbfounded as oral production and interactions with native-English-speaker instructors were difficult, to the point of being almost impossible (Burnaby & Sun, 1989; Goto-Butler, 2004, 2007; Jin & Cortazzi, 1998; Park, 2012).

The educational contexts in Asian countries have largely pushed students to view the EL as a strategic tool for successful preparation for college entrance examinations, and not as a tool to enhance their communication abilities with English teachers (Park, 2012). Proponents of this view believed that to 'train students to pass the entrance exams, teacher's [sic] attention is greatly directed by what is on the exams' (Liu *et al.*, 2004: 704), and that meeting the national and local mandates for obtaining higher examination scores in these countries superseded the need for promoting communicative competence. However, critics of this viewpoint have contended that, in many Asian educational contexts, 'language instruction focused so intently on grammar and translation that students often acquired insufficient communication skills' (Butler, 2004: 245).

The normative curricular regime politically and culturally mandated in these educational contexts could be seen as being far from adequate in terms of enabling their students to learn English for communicative purposes (Simon-Maeda, 2004). In other words, promotion of these normative curricular practices negated students' own life experiences and their critical consciousness about their learning contexts. Saft and Ohara (2004: 145) discuss the need to promote critical pedagogy in the Japanese educational context, where 'an emphasis on rote learning of facts and cultural influences [placed] priority on group dynamics [which] often have students reluctant to speak out in front of their peers'.

While it is important to move away from essentialized views of culture, we cannot negate how individual women have experienced specific behaviors and norms connected with their familial expectations. Furthermore, it is important to highlight the diversity within each woman's experience, including my own. Being cognizant of our prior schooling and cultural experiences assists in understanding the kinds of learning experiences we brought into our US TESOL programs. Specifically, we each came to the US to gain different knowledge and experience (e.g. Shulman, 1987) in what it means to teach English around the world, especially in our native countries. Many view the Western knowledge and ideologies around EL learning and teaching to be the most important answer to their EL education policy in their native countries, without problematizing the coloniality of this knowledge and these practices (Kumaravadivelu, 2003; Motha, 2014). These 'admission to the US TESOL program' seekers desire to take away best teaching practices from the US to their home educational spaces. This is evident in a plethora of work discussing the failed attempts to import the Communicative Approach to non-English-speaking countries and their classrooms (i.e. Goto-Butler, 2004, 2007; Li, 1998; Nunan, 2003) – embracing best practices without understanding the needs of specific learners and the realities of educational contexts. Simply, what has worked in the US would probably not work in other countries, unless specific learners are understood, given their educational milieus. In particular, the work of Kumaravadivelu (1994,

2001, 2003, 2006) focuses on the 'concept of postmethod as an alternative to method rather than an alternative method' (Kumaravadivelu, 2003: 544). Simply, teaching methods need to be re-envisioned and re-conceptualized, since how to teach should truly focus on who the learners are and the context in which learning takes place as one way to be autonomous about the ways in which one learns. As a result, Kumaravadivelu (2001) conceptualizes postmethod pedagogy, which encompasses the parameters of particularity, practicality and possibility. Particularity zooms in on a 'particular group of teachers teaching a particular groups [sic] of learners pursuing a particular set of goals within a particular institutional context embedded in a particular sociocultural milieu' (Kumaravadivelu, 2001: 538). In the practicality parameter, theory-to-practice connection in the local context is critical due to the ways in which local knowledge in global space is often marginalized and taken less serious than global/Western knowledge (Bhattacharya, 2011; Kumaravadivelu, 2003). Furthermore, the parameter of possibility is supported by the work of Paulo Freire's critical pedagogy 'that seeks to empower classroom participants so that they can critically reflect on the social and historical conditions contributing to create the cultural forms and interested knowledge they encounter in their lives' (Kumaravadivelu, 2003: 544). Hence, the three parameters work together to create a rationale for promoting postcolonial teaching practices. Such an emphasis on criticality becomes vital in preparing all teachers to teach English around the world.

I end this chapter with an excerpt from Nuske (2015: 309) regarding exerting our critical endeavors: 'If valued critical objectives are to be achieved and not merely espoused, teacher educators must intensify their own reflective practice and continually monitor the effects of their problem-posing efforts'. As such, it is important for language teachers and teacher educators to be mindful of how we demonstrate criticality in our educational settings. It is only when we begin to share with our students how the notion of criticality has influenced our journeys as language educators that we can begin to integrate these ideas into our professional and pedagogical practices.

More empirical and curricular work is needed on exploring and understanding race–gender–class connections as they relate to issues of privilege and marginalization in the lives of (women) teachers of English. It is only through extending and furthering our work on what it means to coexist in privilege and marginalization as teachers of English, that we can begin to understand the true meaning behind 'creating safe spaces for teacher candidates to wrestle with issues of race, class, gender ...' (refer to the epigraph of this chapter – Varghese et al., 2016: 20).

Notes

(1) With the *Race, Ethnicity and Education* journal editors' permission, sections of this chapter comes from Park (2015).
(2) https://www.iie.org/Research-and-Insights/Open-Doors/Data/International-students/Enrollment-Trends/.
(3) Kachru (1997) also discussed Inner Circle and Outer Circle countries (ICCs and OCCs). ICCs use English as their first and primary language, and OCCs are ones that have been historically colonized by English-dominant countries. It is also important to be mindful that there are inherent challenges with Kachru's concentric circles, for they do not take into consideration those individuals who are transnational, hybrid and multilingual in claiming multiple nationalities and ethnicities when it comes to their linguistic and cultural identities.

3 'Writing *is* a Way of Knowing' in Promoting Evocative-Genres of Inquiry: Methodological Choices[1]

> *All our writing is influenced by our life histories. Each word we write represents an encounter, possibly a struggle, between our multiple past experience and the demands of a new context. Writing is not some neutral activity which we just learn like a physical skill, but it implicates every fiber of the writer's multifaceted being.*
> Ivanic, 1998: 181

I begin this chapter with an excerpt from Roz Ivanic's (1998) *Writing and Identity: The Discoursal Construction of Identity in Academic Writing*, because this book-writing endeavor is a scholarly inquiry that has allowed me to reflect on my own evolution in understanding the importance of writing in constructing my identity. I realized the 'autobiographical self' (Ivanic, 1998: 24) as one avenue for understanding my life history. According to Ivanic, the 'autobiographical self' focuses on connecting identity:

> ... with a writer's sense of their roots, of where they are coming from, and the knowledge that the identity they bring with them to writing is, in itself socially constructed and constantly changing as a consequence of their developing life history... (Ivanic, 1998: 24)

Specifically, I came to see 'autobiographical self' writing as a way to connect critical issues of language learning, teaching and identity (Norton, 2000), as well as a means to create 'more culturally informed and transformative educators' (Hale *et al.*, 2008: 1413). Hence, this connection links my 'autobiographical self' to my 'discoursal self' – the impression of myself, 'often multiple, sometimes contradictory, which [I] consciously or unconsciously present within the contexts which I enter and exit through my writing' (Ivanic, 1998: 25). To this end, this chapter focuses on multiple, interconnected layers of my methodological inquiry. First, I claim my 'autobiographical self' as research instrument. Second, the lessons learned from reflecting on my 'autobiographical self' become a framework for constructing my teacher-scholar identity. Third, I discovered, via autobiographical writing, other forms of evocative genres as methodological and pedagogical tools, enabling me to position myself as a reflective and political researcher.

This subjective positioning has allowed me to understand narrativizing as a process of inquiry in making meanings of our stories (Bell, 2002; Elbaz-Liwisch, 2001; Johnson & Golombek, 2002; Peshkin, 1988; Ramanathan, 2005; Van Manen, 1990). Next, I outline the specific evocative genres of writing that are at the foundation of my work. In this section, I chronicle the data sources (via a flowchart) that have become the heart of this book. I conclude this chapter with discussions around the methodological rigor employed in the study, and ultimately in penning this book.

Claiming my 'Autobiographical Self' as Research Instrument

When I began to construct my own autobiography throughout my doctoral education, every word I scribed became an intense encounter and struggle between 'my past experience and the demand of a new context' (Ivanic, 1998: 181), as I reconstructed my identity as a Korean immigrant girl in the US in the late 1970s, and as a graduate student studying the experiences of diaspora. Hence, my writing became situated, social and political in nature (Gee, 1991; Ivanic, 1998). I found myself writing about being terrified in an elementary classroom full of unfamiliar faces, and not understanding the language and its culture. I struggled with the reading and writing curriculum, which had no connection to my own history, culture or experiences in education up to that point. Through reflecting and writing about my own learning, I came to develop a complex knowledge of the intense connection between my realizations, stemming from my coming to understand what writing pedagogies worked for me as a new student to the US, and also from my reflections on what school practices and situations I struggled with during my first several years of US schooling. Of critical importance to my emerging pedagogy was personal recognition of the underlying belief that every student who entered my classroom had a unique life history, which needed to be privileged in my teaching. Thus, tapping into my life history to chronicle an 'autobiographical self' in order to understand my 'discoursal self' was how I integrated my lived experiences and those of others into my teaching and research. As a consequence, these became a fundamental part of my pedagogical learner knowledge (Shulman, 1987), further allowing me to see my 'self as [teacher-scholar] author' (Ivanic, 1998: 27) in the academy, building strong relationships with my students and the five women who have enriched my life as a teacher-scholar, ultimately penning this book.

Lessons Learned from my 'Autobiographical Self': Constructing my Teacher Scholar Identity

Constructing my autobiographical self was an empowering experience for me in two specific ways. One lesson learned was that learning English was more than the '... mastery of the linguistic code' (Flowerdew & Miller, 2008: 204). It entailed learning about and understanding the world around me through English. In documenting the life history narratives of three engineering graduate students in Hong Kong, Flowerdew and Miller cited the work of Lantolf and Pavlenko (1995: 110) in stating that 'the language acquisition device is not located in the head of the individual but is situated in the dialogic that arises between individuals engaged in goal directed activities'. For me, constructing my autobiographical self was a goal-directed activity that allowed me to see and understand the world around me. This led to the second lesson learned, specifically in coming to understand how my identities around race, gender and class intersected with language. I realized that my identities were largely influenced and (re)shaped by the sociocultural and sociopolitical contexts in which I had lived, and the spaces I traverse now (Freire, 2006; Nieto, 2010; Norton, 2000; Park, 2011, 2013a, 2013b). In the second lesson, my linguistic and racial identity became scrutinized as I navigated the space where Standard English and being white were privileged more often than not. However, with time, I came to embrace my own linguistic identity, which became a powerful tool in constructing my being and in becoming an advocate for myself and other professionals from diverse backgrounds. This began the interrogation of my own privilege that coexists with issues of marginalization.

In addition to lessons learned from constructing my autobiographical self, writing, specifically writing about my own lived experiences, became an evocative inquiry that was both emotional and liberating. With these writing experiences, I was introduced to other forms of evocative genres in doctoral education as methodological and pedagogical tools. These tools were experimented with in my community college courses (2000–2008). As such, my adult, pre-academic English as an additional language students (EALs) were able to experience constructing their own identities via the literacy narrative writing project (refer to Park, 2010, 2011, 2013b for a detailed description of the CLA project). These two lessons allowed me to bring together the ways in which I wanted to frame my inquiry into understanding the lived experiences of the women. These lessons learned also aligned my epistemological perspective with Shohamy's (2004) recommendation, in that my ultimate goal became focused on the question of exploring and understanding women's lived experiences:

> Researchers should not be forced to ask themselves whether they are doing critical ethnography or narrative research...should not feel that they must define their research identity based on such modes...should feel free to examine a variety of modes, to mix and blend different ones in the long journey toward answering research questions... (Shohamy, 2004: 729)

Becoming and Being a Reflexive and Political Researcher in Exploring Women's Stories

As a qualitative researcher focused on exploring each woman's lived experiences, it was critical for me to use a multitude of approaches in getting to the heart of the women's stories. For me, conducting research became a personal and political endeavor that seeks to unpack the ways in which dominant ideology embedded in society influence how we are perceived vis-à-vis one another, as well as others who are unlike us. Embracing this personal and political endeavor meant that I needed to accomplish two things.

First, I desire to interrogate privilege by making an effort to realize the ways in which we (the six of us in this narrative journey) colonize spaces of both marginalization and privilege – it is all about how discourses of privilege intersect with discourses of marginalization (Magnet, 2006; Park, 2015; Vandrick, 2009). In order to accomplish this interrogation, I am reminded of Denzin and Lincoln's (2000: 3) call to situate myself as a 'qualitative bricoleur ... [allowing] research [to be] conducted in a way that is pragmatic, strategic and self-reflexive' (Denzin & Lincoln, 2000: 2). Aligning with Denzin and Lincoln's (2000) call to envision research as a self-reflexive process, Magnet (2006) weaves together a narrative that draws on many conversations during the course of several years, and reveals [her] own position within the complex hierarchy of domination, thus helping herself see that privilege and marginalization coexist. Magnet further claims that self-reflexivity is key to the construction of her narrative, in that 'research is an interactive process shaped by [her] personal history, biography, gender, social class, race and ethnicity' (Denzin & Lincoln, 2000: 4, cited in Magnet, 2006: 737). As such, Magnet (2006: 746) positions her writing to disrupt privilege, and ultimately sees herself as an empowered change agent. In other words, Magnet (2006: 747) calls us to think through the ways in which we are privileged to 'do the hard work of casting aside our own internalized "isms". ... by resisting that there is only one ideology that is liberating – the one in which I am positioned as marginalized'.

Second, my goal is to disrupt the binary war between positivist and interpretivist ways of thinking about conducting research. In other words, conducting research is not about naming the types of paradigm and methodology that one is proposing; it is all about the questions and doubts that one has about the topic at hand (Denzin & Lincoln, 2000; Hendry, 2010; Hesse-Biber & Leavy, 2007; Shohamy, 2004).

Understanding narrative as process of inquiry in making meaning

In my research agenda in general, and in penning this book in particular, I seek multiple ways of understanding our experiences as women traversing different spaces to make meaning around becoming and being teachers of English. Hendry (2010: 79) strongly argues that researchers resituate narrative as inquiry (research) to make meaning of human experience; to continue to interrogate our taken-for-granted; to entertain different ways of being in the world and living with others. As argued by Hendry (2010: 73), conducting research means asking questions: 'At the heart of inquiry is the asking of questions. Inquiry begins with doubt'. I wanted to understand and make sense of what we went (go) through as women from East Asian countries being prepared to be teachers of English to speakers of other languages (TESOL) professionals. Due to the master narratives embedded in the field of who can be ideal English language teachers, I doubted my own existence as an English teacher. I doubted every 'narrative account' of non-white TESOL professionals I came to know in the literature. I wanted to understand the similarities and differences we shared as TESOL professionals from diverse contexts. I desired to make meaning of the pervasive discourses of marginalization that surfaced in the literature. In other words, I wanted to counter those discourses by making meaning around the discourses of privilege that were rarely discussed or interpreted in the lives of TESOL professionals. Hendry (2010: 73) reminds us that, 'our response to question and doubt, in other words the ways in which we organize and make meaning, is narrative'. Furthermore, narrative is a structure for organizing our knowledge and experience (Bruner, 1996, cited in Hendry, 2010: 73). Hence, narrative is a process of understanding and making meaning, and not a method (Hendry, 2010: 73).

Specifically, Hendry contends that symbolic narratives (as separate and distinct from Sacred Narratives and Scientific Narratives) are those that seek to respond to questions of human experience:

> Symbols that seek to re-present human experience are encoded as language (letters), mathematics (numbers), music (notes), space (architecture), and art (form). Symbols do not represent lived experiences, but rather they *interpret* [emphasis my own] experience. In other words, there is no correspondence between reality and the symbol. As Bruner (1996) stated, 'The events recounted in a story take their meaning from the story as a whole. But the story as a whole is something that is constructed from its parts. This part/whole tail-chasing bears the formidable name "hermeneutic circle" and it is what causes stories to be subject to interpretation, not to explanation. Scientific theories or logical proofs are judged based on verifiability or testability; whereas, stories are based on their verisimilitude or "lifelikeness."' (p. 122). (Hendry, 2010: 76)

Symbolic narratives, according to Hendry (2010: 76), uphold multiple ways of interpreting human experiences '... intended to illuminate the whole process of becoming'; as a result, no one method is sufficient. This is also argued and echoed by Shohamy's (2004: 729) statement above, that researchers '... should feel free to examine a variety of modes, to mix and blend different ones in the long journey toward answering research questions'.

While Hendry (2010) views narrative as a process of understanding human experience that embraces multiple ways of knowing, Clandinin and Connelly (2000) see narrative as a form of methodology that pays particular attention to temporality (events are situated in past, present and future), sociality (individual's feelings, hopes, desires, aesthetic reactions and moral dispositions, as well as how these are lived out in contexts; the relationship between the researcher and the researched) and place (physical places where these events take place, which may change given the past, present and future times). However, what they do agree on is that narratives view human experience in which humans, individually and socially, lead to storied lives, in particular, lived experiences – how they are lived (Clandinin & Connelly, 2000; Clandinin et al., 2007).

This is also echoed by Clark and Medina (2000). These authors share their convictions that narratives can open up 'possibilities for multiple meanings and perspectives' (Clark & Medina, 2000: 64), in that narratives serve as powerful tools in understanding how individuals (students, teachers, teacher educators, researchers, administrators, parents, etc.) make meaning of events in their personal and professional lives. Through sharing these narratives in multiple venues, we come to understand the multiple meanings and perspectives that individuals bring to contexts, such as classrooms, programs, etc. In other words, narratives help us to move away from the mindset that there is only one way, or Truth, to understanding our queries. This same conviction was reverberated by Sharma (2015) in her reflective narrative of her journey with reading and writing, in constructing her literacy narrative in graduate education and eventually as a writing teacher in the US. Specifically, Sharma (2015: 108) states that she has come to understand that 'literacy narratives are not just a series of events: More so than other types of narratives, they are frames of meaning that are culturally situated and epistemologically significant'.

Preskill (1998: 346) delineates narrative forms in understanding the narratives of teaching that are at the core of making sense of what it means to teach and prepare teachers to have strong and resilient attitudes toward teaching, and to be mindful of the reason for becoming and being teachers:

Narrative of social criticism helps teachers to critique what is happening in schooling and the larger society.

Narrative of apprenticeship recounts mentoring practices, skills, and strategies that are used by veteran and novice teachers.

Narrative of reflective practice provides opportunity to recount their own practices as teachers and continue to reflect on what it means to teach given specific events that have occurred in their classrooms.

Narrative of journey helps teachers chronicle their career as a whole and their entire life and how teaching has impacted their lives.

Narrative of hope provides us an opportunity to counteract despair – by rediscovering purpose and meaning of education.

Similarly, Pagnucci (2004) advocates for *'Living the Narrative Life'*, looking to *'Stories as a Tool for Meaning Making'* (the title of his book). As I have throughout my academic and professional journey, my research in general, and how I produce research in particular, Pagnucci (2004: 15) argues that 'pursuing narrative scholarship is thus a highly political choice, and a choice that often carries one to the margins of academe'. Just as Hendry (2010) does, Pagnucci (2004: 44) argues that narrative is more than a research methodology – it is a 'way of life', a way of being in the world, '… a set of beliefs. Narrative is ideology'. In this respect, Pagnucci (2004) states the following:

> In exploring the concept of ideology, I wish merely to argue that one's ideology can be focused on a narrative understanding of the world, that once can make the telling and hearing of stories a central part of one's agenda, a central goal that drives one to act in particular ways. (Pagnucci, 2004: 46)

Likewise, Elbaz-Luwisch (2002: 406) argues that 'storying' or 'writing is seen as a process of making meaning. … a method of coming to know'.

In many ways, the argument by these proponent teacher-scholars who empower narrative writing is aligned with the work of Sandra Kouritzin (2000) and her call to bring 'Life to Research'. The 'life' in life history research, according to Kouritzin, calls for further humanizing our research, an approach that allows us to be humans and privilege human experiences in the voices that they choose to tell. For me, the 'life' means being emotional and finding a set of genres that would allow us to be humans and be honest about our feelings. These evocative genres should allow us to combat ideological discourses that are dominant in the Ivory Tower, colonizing our educational and professional spaces with a set of tools for narrative writing that would decolonize the dominant epistemological and ontological perspectives.

Life History Narratives as a Form of Decolonizing Methodological and Pedagogical Approaches

Using life history narratives and other evocative genres of writing (such as autobiography, narrative inquiry, auto-ethnography, life-history narratives, etc.) can be one way to understand the multiple influences that have impacted individuals' lives and career trajectories, especially those from diverse backgrounds. In many ways, promoting these evocative genres of writing to help individuals explore their local knowledge and local contexts can be a form of decolonizing methodological approaches (Lincoln & González y González, 2008). Predominantly, decolonizing methodological approaches foregrounds the stories of experiences or 'voices of nationals or locals (or indigenous peoples)' (Lincoln & González y González, 2008: 784). These approaches allow for 'working with bilingual data, considering non-western cultural traditions, promoting multiple perspectives in texts, and working through technical issues to ensure accessibility' (Lincoln & González y González, 2008: 785).

Furthermore, these approaches can be useful in classroom spaces. As such, English language teaching (ELT) courses promote the use of narrative writing projects as a way to increase EAL students' levels of confidence and fluency in writing, as well as providing teachers the opportunity to be critically reflective (i.e. Carroll *et al.*, 2008; Park, 2008, 2010), thus connecting writing and identity (Ivanic, 1998; Park, 2010, 2011, 2013a, 2013b). In Norton's (2000) seminal work, she explores the experiences of five female Canadian immigrant English as a second language (ESL) students through a longitudinal case-study approach, one that seeks to understand the multiple identities that were constructed and negotiated, based on gender, class and ethnicity. Using interviews and diary studies, Norton reveals the issues of power manifested in their identities as language learners in an unfamiliar Canadian context. The identities of immigrant women and language learners were understood as negotiated within their sociocultural contexts. The immigrant women's identities became even more powerfully visible as writers because they revealed their 'autobiographical, discoursal, and authorial identities' (Norton, 2000: 148). Similarly, but with a different population, research also demonstrates that the use of these evocative genre writing projects in teacher education courses have impacted teacher candidates' decisions to take up a teaching career (i.e. Mawhinney *et al.*, 2012; Margolis, 2008; O'Brien & Schillaci, 2002; Park, 2008, 2009, 2011, 2012, 2013a, 2013b, 2015; Park *et al.*, 2016; Rinke *et al.*, 2014). To this end, research on lived experiences can become a platform for understanding the personal stories that lead to the construction and negotiation of identities.

Following a similar line of genres of writing, Hanauer's (2003, 2010, 2012) work on poetry writing, Hurlbert's (2012) writing as healing and Pavlenko's (2001) work on the bilingual writers' cross-cultural autobiographies all target the heart of exploring writing as meaningful literacy events. These events uncover individuals' lived experiences, complicated by the ways in which issues of social (in)justices impact the ontological and epistemological spaces of individuals. Construction of these meaningful literacy events that unfold our (re)constructed and (re)negotiated identities can begin the process of healing that is often negated and marginalized in publications embraced in higher education. They are meaningful, as the events represent the participants' perspectives (Maxwell, 1996, cited in Hanauer, 2012). Accordingly, by encouraging genres of writing such as autobiography, auto-ethnography, poetry, narrative inquiry and other personal narratives in academia, there is a collective push toward revealing how gendered, racial, linguistic and classed identities have further (dis)enfranchised individuals. More importantly, these genres, as argued by Hanauer (2003: 71), promote 'the experience, concept, and understanding of human diversity', and further, 'present a subjective reworking of the individual's biographical concept and thus allows the researcher an insight into the hidden conceptual and emotional world of the individual' (Hanauer, 2003: 78). Broadly defined, these genres of writing, according to Hanauer (2011: 3), help to foreground human beings and their abilities to make sense of themselves and their surroundings. As such, it is about using participant perspectives (away from possibly skewing the perspectives that a researcher may bring to the experiences of those being studied). Hanauer puts forth Maxwell's (1996) definition of such a process:

> In a qualitative study, you are interested not only in the physical events and behavior that is taking place, but also in how your participants in your study make sense of this and how their understandings influence their behavior ... I am using 'meaning' here in a broad sense to include cognition, affect, intentions, and anything else that can be included in what qualitative researchers often refer to as the 'participant's perspective'. (Maxwell, 1996: 17, cited in Hanauer, 2011: 3)

Chronicling the Data of Our Voices and Experiences: The Four Phases

Figure 3.1 chronicles the data of our voices and experiences. **The first phase** depicts my autobiographical writings since early 2000, when I commenced my doctoral work at University of Maryland, College Park. These autobiographical writings were completed between 2000 and 2006 as part of course assignments, research projects collaborated with faculty and other doctoral students and portions of teaching materials at the community college. **The second phase** covers a period of time I spent with each woman (Han Nah, Liu, Xia, Yu Ri and Shu-Ming). I got to know each woman through their rendering of their autobiographical writings chronicling their journeys from their native countries to matriculating into their US TESOL programs. I also had individual interviews spanning a period of 12 months (two to three times per month) for most of them, and about 15 months for Han Nah (a weekly interview). Finally, most of the women shared their journal entries of critical incidents experienced

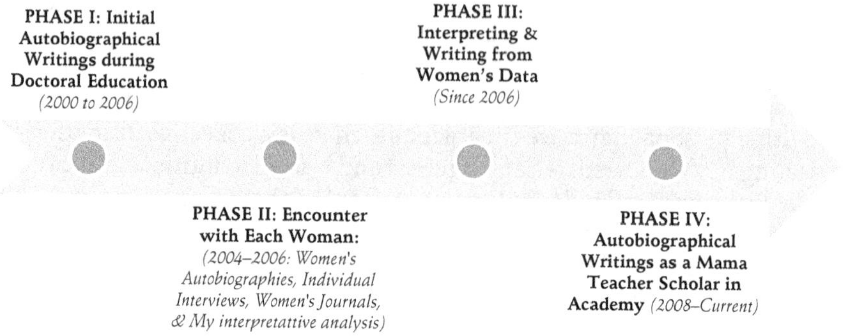

PHASE I: Initial Autobiographical Writings during Doctoral Education *(2000 to 2006)*

PHASE II: Encounter with Each Woman: *(2004–2006: Women's Autobiographies, Individual Interviews, Women's Journals, & My interpretattive analysis)*

PHASE III: Interpreting & Writing from Women's Data *(Since 2006)*

PHASE IV: Autobiographical Writings as a Mama Teacher Scholar in Academy *(2008–Current)*

Figure 3.1 Flowchart of data source phases

during their matriculation in the TESOL programs. The **third phase** focuses on a time period between completing my PhD, obtaining a tenure-track position and becoming a mom. Specifically, during these two years, I focused not only on becoming a mom, but also on trying to publish from my dissertation research data. As a result, I interacted with each woman's data more intimately to find academic homes for their stories, coupled with being current with published work in my field. **The final phase** zooms in on my experiences at the current institution as a mama scholar in academy.

While Figure 3.1 seems linear in its visual depiction, it is important to note that these time periods are interconnected, and complicate and reinforce one another as I make sense of our lived experiences in penning this book. Within each section and across the four sections, I focused on coding for theoretical constructs that delineate connections among race–gender–class, and how those intersect with EL teaching. In privileging these constructs, I came to understand further the coexistence of privilege and marginalization in our lived experiences. Hence, my data sources depicted in this flowchart, coupled with my data analysis of coding for specific theoretical constructs, are part of recurring and dialogic process. It is through interacting and dialoging with each woman, along with my critical reflections of my journey, that I am able to pen this book.

The beginning of interactive and dialogic process

I progressed through the writing of this book in an 'interactive dialogic manner that required self-disclosure on the part of researcher [which] encouraged reciprocity' (Lather, 1991: 60). For many reasons, both known and unknown to us, it was very difficult to get the women engaged in discussing their experiences during the first couple of sessions. I felt that I needed to share with them a piece of my own history in order to present myself as an ethical researcher embarking on a study of the lived experiences of the six of us. The fact that I also shared my own experiences with these women helped me to (1) get closer to them as other human beings; and (2) open up their experiences in my presence to understand their histories as lived. These characteristics are consistent with Frank's (2012) call to embrace what it means to practice dialogic narrative work. This is also echoed in Weinstein's (2004: 111) offer of a curriculum entitled *Learners' Lives as Curriculum*, built on the premise that 'teachers must listen for learner stories to discover the most pressing issues that will bring language learning to life'. In this community, Weinstein (2004: 119) created space where 'both her model [teachers] and her willingness to participate as an equal created the trust that enabled reluctant strangers to become participants ... teachers participated in the community they were creating in the classroom'. Weinstein (2004: 119) also saw herself as learner, in that 'like any learner, she also needed time within and across programs to tell stories about teaching and to compare and analyze [her own] experiences'.

'Stories within STORIES'

> Stories are always told within dialogues: Storytelling responds to others – whether actually present or imagined – and anticipates future responses, including the retelling of the story, with variations. (Frank, 2012: 33)

All of the data collected from the women (Han Nah, Liu, Xia, Yu Ri and Shu-Ming) were understood and experienced as dialogues. Frank (2012: 34) argues that 'any individual voice is actually a dialogue between voices'. In other words, dialogic process encompasses individuals carrying on their dialogue as well as the 'generalized others of a speech community, not specific individuals' (Frank, 2012: 35). In particular, for the women and myself, our stories were not only about how we traverse as nonnative English speaker (NNES) women teachers of English in multiple educational spaces, but also about decolonizing the grand narratives depicting the societal-level discourses that privilege and marginalize individuals in our TESOL profession. These societal-level discourses are depicted in the work of Barkhuizen (2016: 655) as 'STORIES' that are part of individual 'stories and Stories'. Similarly, Frank (2012: 36) argues that, 'We humans are able to express ourselves only because so many stories already exist for us to adapt, and these stories shape whatever sense we have of ourselves'. These existing stories for us point to the dominant ideology that places women, NNESTs and teaching English in a certain sphere, in that only certain individuals with specific characteristics – middle-class, white race, accent-free speech, able-bodied and heterosexual – are embraced. Finally, in adhering to the dialogical narrative analysis work, I, as a co-participant as well as the storyteller of our stories, have to be open to 'continuing possibilities of listening and of responding to what is heard' (Frank, 2012: 37). It is also about embracing the unfinishedness (Freire, 1998) as well as 'unfinalizability' (Bahktin, 1984) of our stories, which point to the probability that the stories that we choose to (re)tell throughout this book 'will instigate more stories ...' (Frank, 2012: 49), being mindful that stories are 'representations not so much of life as it is, but of life as it is imagined, with that imagination shaped by previous stories' (Frank, 2012: 50).

The women's stories via 'reflective, dialogic or performative interviews': Disclosing the issues of trustworthiness, credibility and ethics of doing narrative work

I followed Denzin's (2001: 24) new form of the interview, called 'reflexive, dialogic, or performative interview', that brings us together into a moral community. In what follows, Denzin argues for a moral community building:

> It is not a commodity that you hire someone to collect for you, or that you pay someone to give you. ... As researchers, we belong to a moral community. Doing interviews is a privilege granted to us, not a right that we have. Interviews are things that belong to us. Interviews are part of the dialogic conversation that connects all of us to this larger moral community. Interviews arise out of performance events. They transform information into shared experience. I imagine a world where race, ethnicity, class, gender and sexual orientation intersect; a world where language and performance empower, and humans can become who they wish to be, free of prejudice, repression and discrimination. (Denzin, 2001: 24)

In upholding the grounds of this moral community, I often questioned the academic discourse community in which writing this book has now positioned me. As a teacher, scholar and writer from a hybrid space – interconnections of cultures and languages of Self and Other (Ha, 2008), I often felt, similarly to those from other linguistic spaces who write academically, silenced through my writing due to the 'foreignness' I lived in my own writing in US academia (Viete & Ha, 2007: 41). Even with this feeling of silenced-ness, I asked questions related to the women's prior educational experiences in their native countries, in order to understand their English language and cultural learning experiences leading up to admissions into TESOL programs in the US. Furthermore, I probed into how they imagined their futures to be upon completion of US TESOL programs. The women's responses to these interview questions became part of my life as well, a life I lived through, wrestled with, and the life I advocate for as a TESOL professional, woman, teacher scholar, researcher and mother in academia. In many ways, this internal process of being silenced by US academia pushed me to continue to journey through and to influence and be influenced by our moral community. Just as Viete and Ha (2007) articulated:

> [R]eading and writing are social acts that are often in essence political in that they incorporated relations of power. Academic research discourses are no exception. They play out the politics of knowing (who knows what; who can say what; how we can say it) and politics of presenting knowledge (who knows how to argue, reference, be relevant, in specific ways). They also participate in the politics of English as a global language, where power (or superiority) is conferred through knowing how to use English in particular ways. (Viete & Ha, 2007: 41)

Even with this knowledge of power inherent in ultimately writing this book in English, my goal is to share with others in similar epistemological camps what it means to navigate the identity politics – my own as well as those of the women who entered my life – to uphold the power that comes with shared knowledge, stories and experiences. It was within our power-driven, interactive, collective stories that I arrived at a fuller understanding (which is still unfinished) of how they had experienced, and might continue to experience, the ELT enterprise vis-à-vis their identity constructions and negotiations.

Interpretation and organization of women's stories: Data presentation

All five women came from varying degrees of privileged class backgrounds. These backgrounds were marked by the fact that they were introduced to English language learning at early ages, and given ample financial and other supports to embark on study abroad programs geared toward completion of advanced degrees. Due to their privileged class backgrounds, these women came both to learn in and to associate with different communities of practice, as sites of cultural and linguistic learning (Lave & Wenger, 1991). With cultural and symbolic capital under their belts, they gained admission into TESOL programs in the US, with the intent of living out their imagined future identities as language specialists (Bourdieu & Passeron, 1977).

As a researcher, my goal was to let the five women's narratives speak to me in ways that would not confine the narratives and the theorizing of narratives into one theoretical framework or methodological approach (Shohamy, 2004). As has been stated by many scholars studying identity construction, understanding teachers' identities can be a complex endeavor, and it can be further complicated when the teachers come from different educational, linguistic, social, cultural and political terrains, as was the case in my study (Norton, 2000; Pavlenko, 2003; Varghese *et al.*, 2005, 2016). My crafting of the women's narratives represents one of many possible ways of interpreting how these women came to understand their identities in relation to their past, present and future experiences within the English language learning and teaching enterprise.

The women's narratives highlight a series of events that mark past, present and future in general, and language learning experiences in home countries, entering the US TESOL programs, and events experienced throughout their time in the US in particular. As such, the narrative events depicted in this book are their unfinished (Freire, 1998) life histories. For each woman, this explication serves as an unfinished life history, as further follow-up interviews might reveal other perspectives and revelations that may not have been highlighted in the study. As stated in the beginning of the book, I privilege how Shu-Ming's and my life journeys interlace in a different scholarly venue as a result of how I perceive my identities vis-à-vis those of Shu-Ming. Making this very decision was complex and difficult, for I do not want Shu-Ming, nor the readers, to see this decision as an act of marginalization of Shu-Ming.

It is important to understand that the construct of identities cannot be, nor should it be, compartmentalized into past–present–future life history timelines due to the fluid, multiple and contesting nature of these women's identities (Norton, 2000). These three different but interconnected time periods might be construed as being fragmented; however, I stress this timeline in order to help me make connections with respect to the changing nature of their identities within their past, present and future ELT contexts. Each woman brought forth a unique narrative highlighting her East Asian background, as reflected in the stories re-storied by me. Additionally, they portrayed grand narratives – stories that were told from the perspectives of learners and teachers, incurring both challenges and victories in TESOL (Norton, 2000; Pavlenko, 2004). Although the women's narratives have been constructed in a parallel manner, some women's narratives will be more extensive than others due to variations in their lived experiences. Their narratives are symbolic of resistance to 'essentialist ways of thinking about the experiences of [NNES or East Asian] women as fundamentally alike, a homogeneous group with common life opportunities and experiences already known to us before we actually see them or hear from them' (Harding, 1996: 432).

To uphold this resistance, it was important for me, as a researcher and colleague, to share with the five women, as well as the readers, as much as I could about their stories. Personal narratives come from within, and it was the choice of these women to share more or less with me as the researcher. In turn, I made choices to narrate these stories as I heard them and felt them, as both an insider and outsider to the lives of my participants (Harding, 1987; Haroian-Guerin, 1999; Ladson-Billings, 2000; Van Manan, 1988). As a result, each woman's stories of race, gender and class intersecting with the English language and framed within the past–present–future timeline were further organized around themes centering around how issues of privilege and marginalization coexisted for each woman that mattered to each woman at the time of data collection. For instance, Han Nah, as the only married woman with children at the time of data collection, focused more on how her gender identities privileged or marginalized her professional and linguistic identities, the focus of Chapter 4. On the other hand, for Liu, Xia and Yu Ri, the larger narrative at the time of data collection was to understand their teacher identity given how they positioned themselves linguistically and racially as East Asian women in TESOL, the focus of Chapter 5. Now I turn to these chapters.

Note

(1) With the *ELT* journal editors' permission, sections of this chapter come from Park (2013b).

4 Where Privilege Meets Marginalization in Han Nah's Lived Experiences: Navigating her Multiple Gendered Identities[1]

My father thought that if I study [Turkish language and Islamic studies], it would be good for my career ... He thinks that I cannot compete with men in Korean society. I should work in a very unique area that nobody else does to be successful in my life ... (Interview, 1/21)

[My mother said,] if women live very happily, they do not need to work. Being a housewife is good with a high status man ... [according to my mother,] I can't study because [I] have to take care of my children. (Interview, 4/9)

I had to choose whether to [return] to Turkey [to finish my PhD program] or come to the United States with [my husband] ... I listened to my mom and kind of my society. I always heard that women should follow [their husbands]. I had to have a baby to keep my family to continue. (Interview, 1/21)

I really want to speak English very well, and then I can practice my English with my children, but I don't want my children to only speak English. So I always speak Korean at home, and then I don't have that many American friends outside because I am really busy at home with my children ... (Interview, 1/4)

Now, I am a Korean [language] instructor. And then, in the future, I want to work for the Koreans in the US ... I want the children to speak both languages [Korean and English fluently]. ... I want my children to become kind of international, knowing both Korean and English languages as well as culture ... (Interview, 1/4)

The above excerpts largely illuminate the ways in which Han Nah navigates and negotiates her identities as a daughter, spouse and mother, and later connecting her mothering identity to her language teacher identity in the US. Though Han Nah was showered with privilege in the sense of having the resources to access a variety of educational spaces during college and graduate education, her gendered position in both her family and community compromised her position of power and limited her ability to realize her imagined future identities as a Korean-Turkish scholar. Hence, the focus of this chapter is to highlight the ways in which I interpreted Han Nah's journey in wrestling with her multiple gendered identities. Moreover, through this analysis work, I began to make sense of the unfolding of my own lived experiences as a daughter, spouse, teacher educator and mama scholar in the academy. In particular, I attempt to entertain the question posed by the work of post-structuralists such as Judith Butler and Bonnie Norton, 'How did gender come to make a difference?' in our lives as women traversing different contexts (Higgins, 2010: 373). Would we have had the same experiences if we were men?

In this chapter, I privilege gender as a lens to unfold our lived experiences, especially Han Nah's. More importantly, through this chapter, I argue that 'women's experiences need to be understood not only at the institutional level but also at the personal level. Women's familial experiences are conditioned by the social and familial structure and are also related to their gendered desire' (Lee & Park, 2001). However, I am also mindful that 'research that examines gender as a complex system of social relations does not seek to make generalizations about gendered experiences, nor does it strive to predict how individuals may experience [other identity constructions] based on other individuals' experiences' (Higgins, 2010: 374). Hence, sharing bits and pieces of my own history is a result of my own reflections as I re-read my narrative rendition of Han Nah's experiences.

'[My father] thinks that I cannot compete with men in Korean society': Promoting Gender Equity for His Daughter?

Han Nah's experience learning English in Korea was primarily focused on doing well on college entrance examinations; as a result, she did not have enough opportunities to practice English orally. While in college, she was attracted to watching news and people debating current events on TV, because at that time, she said, '[I] wanted to be a kind of Korean–English interpreter. So [I] prepared for that career' (Interview, 1/6). All her hopes were focused on passing the interpretation examination sponsored by the only interpretation and translation school in Korea. But in 1992, her dream of becoming a translator ended when she was not able to pass the entrance examination. Not wanting to go through additional long years of entrance examination preparation, she decided to enter a graduate program to pursue Turkish language and Islamic women's studies in 1992.

For Han Nah, selecting Turkish studies as her major was ultimately the decision of her father. Han Nah's father dictated what the best area of specialization would be for her future. Her father believed that women needed to choose a major that was viewed as special in Korea, as there was fierce competition among men and women to secure a promising career upon graduating from college.

> [M]y father thought that if I study [these] special things, it would be good for my career. In Korea, students' parents have full responsibilities, for their college life, so parents' influence is really huge. He wanted me to have a success in my life. (Interview, 1/21)

In addition to the above rationale, Han Nah noted that there was another reason why her father wanted her to pursue Turkish studies as her major, which had much to do with her gendered identity and the societal-level discourse pervasive in a Korean patriarchal society.

> He thinks that I cannot compete with men in Korean society. I should work in a very unique area that nobody else does to be successful in my life ... At that time, I did not understand quite much but because my father supported my college education, I just agreed ... [My father] thinks that men can actually do anything he wants if he tries to do it, so my brother chose his major to be Economics because he was interested [in it.] My first sister's major was biology, but my father suggested pharmacy, but she really wanted to do biology. After college, she really regret about it. Though my sister was in the top of her class, the only way she could continue in biology was to keep studying to get a PhD to become a professor, or any other area [would be] hard. (Interview, 1/21)

Although Han Nah was saddened by the fact that her father did not believe she could compete with men, she viewed this as a part of reality for women living in Korean society. In the above excerpt, she discussed her brother's choice to go into economics and a sister's choice to go into biology. Her father's support for her brother had always been there, but he did not agree with her sister's choice to be a biologist. Her father's suggestion that her sister go into pharmacy as opposed to biology and his choice of a major for Han Nah in Turkish language and Islamic studies had much to do with the fact that they both were to be married and both were to have families during their professional career years, which was also in alignment with what Korean society's normative expectation was of women (Lee & Park, 2001; Li & Beckett, 2006). The fact that it is possible for his daughters to remain single and be experts in their disciplinary fields was not even in his mindset; it did not fit with how women should be in his cultural framework. Since Han Nah was highly dependent on her parents for economic stability, she did everything they asked her to do, from selecting her college major to going 'to graduate school and [going] abroad to study' (Interview, 4/19). All in all, her father's advice to her and her sisters was always to be in a unique major or profession dominated by women and not men, so that they did not have to compete with other men when it came to 'taking a leave of absence' to get married and have a family.

In many ways, Han Nah's father could be seen as a realist, wanting Han Nah to understand the structural inequality embedded in Korean sociocultural and sociopolitical contexts. As I write this book and revisit Han Nah's narratives, I can't help but think about my own relationship with my parents when it came to my career paths. While I did not have the luxury of studying in multiple countries throughout my K–16 contexts, my parents wanted the best for me. The 'best' equated with studying to become a medical doctor. My parents were convinced that I would become a medical doctor one day, and this thinking went on for several years until I fell in love with teaching English serendipitously. Just as I was influenced by my parents' mindset about my singular career path of becoming a medical doctor, Han Nah was just as influenced by her parents.

Han Nah's father had a lot of influence on her decision-making processes as they related to her gendered identities. He had been the driving force in determining the majors for her undergraduate and graduate programs. Was Han Nah's father promoting gender equity for his daughter so that she, too, could be a legitimate central participant in a competitive world dominated by men? Or, as Judith Butler would put it, was he further subjugating Han Nah to perform her gendered identity? Han Nah's father, though contradicting the normative parental behaviors in Korea and other Asian countries, could be interpreted as providing his daughter with a sense of purpose in her own learning trajectory. Another way to interpret his perspectives would be that he knows that Han Nah would have to forego her future when she became a married woman with children.

Han Nah's gender positioning by her father placed her in a pool to be competitive with other men, and in a very unique and unpopulated scholarship opportunity as well, which might require the disciplinary committee to keep Han Nah to promote gender equity in academic programs. Just as Liu's parents wanted her to become a teacher for reasons that were largely related to her gender and the competitiveness that would underscore some of the male-dominated positions, Han Nah's father's rationale for choosing this major for Han Nah was similar. First, he did not believe that Han Nah would survive in a major that was popular, since there would be fierce competition both to do well in her classes and to secure employment upon completion of a college degree. Second, by choosing to study Turkish and Islamic studies in her co-educational university, she would be the best among all women pursuing a college education, since her major was unique and women were rarely seen studying in this field. Moreover, her father's belief was that women, too, could be independently professional, and that they did not need to rely on their husbands to make them economically and professionally secure. In reality, Han Nah's father's decision for her to major in Turkish and Islamic studies, and his belief that women could be independent, were paradoxical with respect to that which was prescribed by Korean society, because the society not only devalued women but it also perceived women to be dependent on men: on their father when single, on their husband when married and on their sons when elderly, according to Confucian philosophy.

'I thought I had to [serve coffee] because I was a woman': Han Nah's Assigned Identities in Korean Higher Education

Even within the Turkish studies field in Korea, Han Nah felt marginal due to her gender. Han Nah also felt inferior due to her gendered experiences. Han Nah reminisced about the days when she was an academic assistant for a director of Middle East studies in graduate school in Korea. Han Nah was among several academic and research assistants working in the Middle East studies department, but she was the only woman graduate student. She stated that her professor always wanted Han Nah to serve guests coffee instead of asking male students to do so. While she thought it was odd that she was the only student serving coffee, 'I thought I had to do it because I was a woman' (Interview, 3/15). This is a perfect example of how being in a disciplinary program unpopulated by women could further subjugate Han Nah and, in essence, she was compelled to 'perform' her gendered actions.

At that time, she accepted this role as part of being in an academic setting working under her professor, and she did not view it as gender inequity. '[I]t's acceptable. It is not just a relationship between men and women, kind of relationship between professors and students. This is also a Confucian type philosophy; he is my professor; he is also my elder, so I have to do something for him' (Interview, 3/15). She equated the serving of her male professors and male students with Korean social norms, and it was something that occurred at her own home as well. Han Nah and her sisters helped their mother with household chores while her brother and father were recipients of what was served. In this way, Han Nah viewed her professional setting as an extension of her home environment, which was her justification.

'[My Turk professors] never expected me to do kind of research ...': Han Nah's Assigned Identities in Turkish Higher Education

During graduate school in Korea, Han Nah envisioned herself as a professor working in Korea but researching Middle East studies, with an emphasis on Turkish women. By studying in Turkey and specializing in Islamic women's issues, she hoped to bring new and enlightening perspectives into the Korean higher educational system. This prompted her to continue studying this field, in a PhD program in Turkey, upon completion of her master's in Korea in 1994. She believed that living in a Turkish society among Islamic women would help her understand their experiences firsthand. 'I just wanted to research on Turkish women, working women. In Korea, there are lots of discrimination and they cannot be promoted in companies, I just wanted to know if there were these kinds of things in Turkey' (Interview, 1/21).

Even though Han Nah didn't have to serve coffee in the academic setting as was the case in her university in Korea, Turkish professors' expectations of her as a doctoral student were low. Because Han Nah was one of few Asians studying in Turkey, her Turkish professors and peers saw her as a marginal member, who could never be a full-fledged member of the Turkish scholarship community. Hence, it was easy for Han Nah to study, since all she had to focus on was her Turkish language proficiency.

> [My Turk professors] did not expect that much. They never expected me to do kind of research. They always thought that I may go back to Korea some day and it does not matter if I did something in Turkey. I had low motivation and kind of agreed with them in that I am going back to Korea, and I am going to do something in Korea, not in Turkey. (Interview, 2/8)

Just as Han Nah never saw herself as a part of the Turkish community, her Turkish professors assigned a specific set of racial and linguistic identities on Han Nah – a non-Turkish woman traveler, an outsider. As such, Turkish professors and Turk doctoral students undervalued her educational potential as a scholar. They saw her as an outsider in relation to what she could accomplish in the Turkish educational setting as a PhD student. Due to this 'assigned' set of identities on Han Nah in Turkey, she only focused on improving her Turkish language proficiency (Varghese et al., 2005). Her professors and colleagues in Turkey saw her as a person who would return to Korea some day. Her participation in the Turkish scholarly community was therefore marginal as opposed to legitimately peripheral, a movement toward intense participation in the community (Lave & Wenger, 1991).

Hence, Han Nah never questioned her status in Turkey, and took their labeling of her as a legitimate identity, since she also agreed that she would one day return to Korea to expand Korean knowledge of Turkish Islamic studies. Moreover, Han Nah had no intention of marrying within the Turkish community (Kinginer, 2004; Norton, 2000, 2001). All in all, Turkish scholars within her PhD program, who were themselves Turkish, positioned her as an outsider in the scholarly community due to her ethnic and racial identity as a Korean woman who would eventually return to Korea. This paralleled Norton and Pavlenko's (2004: 4) statement that our 'access to and distribution of resources may be at times both racialized and gendered'. More importantly, Han Nah's experiences in the Middle East Institute in Korea as well as her PhD program in Turkey illustrate how her 'access to the target language and culture is mediated by gendered identities and other forces including power differentials, race, [language] ... and cultural differences between ... differing communities' (Higgins, 2010: 376).

'Because you are a married woman ...': Married and Bound by her Native Cultural Norms

As racial, linguistic and gendered marginalization ensued in Turkish contexts for Han Nah, her mother urged her to leave her PhD program in Turkey, to immigrate to the US with her husband: '[B]ecause you are a married woman, you never live separately ... I always heard that women should be this way. I had to have a baby to keep my family to continue' (Interview, 1/4). Han Nah's decision to perform her gendered identities, as consistent with Korean societal norms and her mother, led her to leave the PhD program in Turkey to care for her husband and start a family. Han Nah's parents believed that due to her age (in Korean society, a woman's age of 25 is perceived as advanced), she needed to have children as soon as she got married. Given these expectations, Han Nah abandoned her area of expertise. Her newly claimed identity as a married woman brought her to the US to be with her student husband. Han Nah stated,

> I had to choose whether I had to stay in Turkey [to finish my PhD program] or come [to the United States] with him. [B]ecause you are a married woman, you never live separately. So I listened to my mom and kind of my society. I always heard that women should be this way. I had to have a baby to keep my family to continue. (Interview, 1/4)

Han Nah noted that for her, getting married and moving to the US changed her life trajectory; but having children and thinking about her imagined future gendered identities as a spouse and mother further changed her identities, and she began to negotiate her future lived experiences as a professional Korean woman with children.

There were other occasions where Han Nah had to forego her learning opportunities due to her gendered responsibilities – her claiming of a gendered identity as a mother. She had to discontinue taking intensive English language courses and other sociology research courses due to her pregnancies. She stated, 'I could not keep studying because no one helped me to take care of the children and housework' (Interview, 1/4). In essence, what Han Nah experienced in terms of not having enough help with raising her children and continuing her education was similar to what Japanese EFL students shared in Saft and Ohara's (2004) study. The Japanese women shared that they could not pursue their career as well as rearing their children. An example of what these women shared is as follows: 'I want to keep working even after I get married, but it will only be possible if my partner helps me. I hope he can do that, but I don't know if I can find such a person' (Saft & Ohara, 2004: 151). Giving up her dream and focusing on the needs of a husband and children was echoed in Lee and Park's (2001) study of Korean women's challenges in their gender roles given the privileging roles of husband, children and parents-in-law.

Ironically, Han Nah's mother did not help her daughter to live out her professional goals, since she was always imposing traditional gender identities on her daughter. Her mother wanted Han Nah to adhere to Korean societal norms with respect to the expected roles for women in Korean society, namely caring for their children and husbands.

> If women live very happily, she does not need to work. Being a housewife is good with a high status man … You can't study because you have to take care of your children. Who is going to take care of your children? (Interview, 4/19)

The above excerpts illustrate Norton and Pavlenko's (2004) notion that 'gender access to linguistic and interactional [other educational] resources' were hampered by Han Nah's mother's traditional dictates. Mothers such as Han Nah's were 'culturally required to be home with [their] children and prioritize their roles as housekeepers, mothers, wives, and caretakers' (Norton & Pavlenko, 2004: 4). This was also consistent with Weis' (1988: 132, cited in Simon-Maeda, 2004) notion of 'socialization process in which women consider marriage and child rearing to be top or sole priorities in their lives without serious consideration of alternative default options'. Similarly, Lee and Park (2001: 16) found that children were the first priority for married women. Han Nah listened to the voices of her mother and Korean societal norms to pave her way for her future directions.

Ultimately, Han Nah chose the path that traditional Korean society had set forth for a married woman, which was to be with her husband

and continue the legacy of her husband's family. This supportive, 'spousal' identity is constructed in relation to 'societal-level discourses' that legitimate and empower identities in Western society (Warriner, 2004: 280) as well as non-Western society. Furthermore, this transition made by Han Nah's husband further shaped *what field, where and how* Han Nah would continue her educational and professional lives in the US. *What field* entailed Han Nah going from English language learner to Korean language teacher as a result of a change to her husband's visa status. *Where* constituted living in New York at the beginning of their immigration, and moving to Atlantic University due to her husband's transfer of his MA program. *How* constituted her husband's visa status changing from that of student to that of US employee, which opened more opportunities for Han Nah, such as matriculating in a degree program as well as finding paid teaching positions. Largely, Han Suk's (Han Nah's husband) educational and professional trajectory became a deciding factor in Han Nah's educational and professional identities, which could be further interpreted as being part of Han Nah's gendered practices as a second-class citizen since her professional aspirations took a back seat to her husband's aspirations. This was also echoed in the work of Warriner (2004) and McClure (2014) where the immigrant women's lives were largely determined in relation to their husbands' positions and other responsibilities they incurred as women living in Western contexts. Another interpretation could be that given the resources Han Nah had, she constructed her identities as best she could.

'[B]ut I don't want my children to only speak English, so I always speak Korean at home...': Connecting Mothering Identity to Her Dominant Language Identity

In 2001, when Han Suk's visa status changed due to his transitioning from that of an international graduate student to a permanent employee of an international organization based in the US, Han Nah's newly claimed visa status allowed her to establish a working status in the US.[2]

> When I had G-4 visa, my status was totally different. That made me a totally different woman. Post 9-11, spouses of [international students] F-2 visa cannot get a degree in the States. So they cannot study, they cannot work, they just have to stay at home. Lot of women have their own career when they were in Korea, but when they came to U.S., their situation totally changed. They feel that they are nothing, just prepare some foods for her husband three times a day, clean the house, no friend, no car, it is really sad ... After I got G-4 visa, I could find a job. (Interview, 2/15)

In trying to secure a job suitable for herself, Han Nah searched on the internet, and realized that there were limited job opportunities for her because of her status as a 'foreigner'. She came to the conclusion that there were only two options for her to work in the US. The first option was to do simple office/administrative work in the Korean-American commerce community, and the second option was to use her specialized skills to work in America, as discussed below:

> [A]fter my husband entered the company, my visa status changed to G4, that means that I could work. After that I tried to find a job, so I searched on the Internet, and I realized that I could not work anywhere because I am a foreigner, don't have any specific skills, so it was really hard for me to work in the U.S. ... So there were two options. Just kind of simple office job working for Korean in Korean society or with my specific skills, work in the U.S. company. Korean [language] is my specific skill for me. (Interview, 2/1)

With this newfound visa and professional direction, Han Nah began to construct new identities, negotiating around her imposed identities as a visible minority woman in an English-speaking context, a mother with two bilingual children being educated in English-only US classrooms, and a spouse whose professional identity rested on her husband's employment location. Han Nah stated that as long as her husband held his position at his current international organization, she would be content to remain in the US, teaching the Korean language, ultimately pursuing her PhD, in bilingual education, and initiating a bilingual school for Korean-American children in the US.

'Now, I am a Korean [language] instructor ...': Claiming Legitimate Linguistic and Professional Identities

As Han Nah's husband's professional trajectory in the US became stable, Han Nah's goal was to work on legitimizing her professional identity coupled with her mothering identity. Menard-Warwick (2004: 307) echoed the choices mothers make in relation to language use and a professional path, in that a woman's investment is 'often strongly connected to family roles and gendered identities, such as motherhood'. Similarly, Mills (2004: 164) also stated that 'a mother's language choices are related to her notions of mothering'. Furthermore, in the excerpt below, Han Nah shared her struggles with accommodating her children in their schooling in English and resisting the dominance of the English language that would benefit the children's identities as Korean-Americans in the Western context. By foregrounding her children's needs, she claimed a dominant linguistic and racial identity, living in and out of her dual linguistic and racial identities as a visible minority, nonnative English speaker (NNES):

> I really want to speak English very well, and then I can practice my English with my children, but I don't want my children to only speak English. So I always speak Korean at home, and then I don't have that many American friends outside because I am really busy at home with my children ... (Interview, 3/15)

Her language choice at home as a mother of two bilingual children and an NNES professional living in and out of the Korean-American contexts played an important role in how she wanted to be perceived in the professional world. Han Nah claimed a dominant linguistic and racial identity as a Korean language teacher in the US. One of the major factors in Han Nah's claiming of dominant linguistic and racial identities in the US was for the benefit of her children born and raised in the US as Korean-Americans. As a result, Han Nah opted to teach her native tongue (Korean) in the US, in order to claim stronger linguistic and cultural identities. She shared the following ideas in one of our interviews:

> Now, I am a Korean [language] instructor. And then, in the future, I want to work for the Koreans in the U.S. ... I want the children to speak both languages [Korean and English fluently]. Most of the [Korean] parents in the U.S. are really busy. They can not spend a lot of time with their children to study Korean. I think we have to make some systematic Korean, kind of a bilingual school for Korean/English, like Spanish/English. ... I want my children to become kind of international, knowing both Korean and English languages as well as culture. (Interview, 1/4)

She believed that this choice would not only benefit her career in the US, but it would also benefit her children growing up as bilinguals. Han Nah's desire for her children and other Korean-American children living in the US to claim their national, heritage identity as well as a transnational identity, traversing both Korean and US borders, became evident. This was echoed in Higgins' (2010: 379) chapter highlighting that 'many parents become concerned with maintaining their children's linguistic and cultural heritage ...'.

In thinking about her amended (or abridged) professional aspiration, Han Nah chose to go into a field that would ultimately benefit her children as well as herself in claiming her dominant linguistic and racial identities in the US. However, this same profession would not benefit her or her children in Korean society, since she was not trained to be a Korean language teacher. As Bourdieu would argue, Han Nah's Korean language teaching skills would be devalued in the Korean educational milieu. This profession, in Korea, was relegated to people who graduated from teachers' colleges. Her decision to teach the Korean language in a higher education institution, as well as in private language institutes subsidized by the government, proved not only to benefit her children, but also herself in the US. For Han Nah, she realized through this work that she could hold down a professional position without feeling linguistically or racially marginalized. This past–present–future trajectory of returning to Han Nah's mother tongue to re-establish her professional identity could be seen as promoting her dominant linguistic image and assisting her with the rearing of her children to be fluent bilingual speakers, so as to enable them to live between Korea and the US (Kanno, 2003; Kouritzin, 2000; Shin, 2014; Vandrick, 2011). Han Nah's desire to maintain her dominant linguistic and racial identities was also aligned with her 'mothering' identity (Mills, 2004), since she desired that her children be fluent bilinguals and 'be international people who can live in Korea and the United States' (Interview, 1/4). Her gendered identity as a wife and a mother changed her life trajectory. Upon exiting the Turkish scholarly community, she felt that she needed to be in a community where she could fulfill the roles of a mother and a professional. Han Nah's negotiated identities were similar to mothers interviewed by Mills (2004) in studying the reasons for mother tongue maintenance. One of the mothers in the study responded, 'I've had two reasons, for the children and for myself' (Mills, 2004: 179). For Han Nah, her coming back to teach the Korean language as opposed to teaching English or Turkish played a salient role in how she desired to be positioned, and how she positioned herself within the dominant society.

'I [did not] come into TESOL to learn how to teach English, but how to teach foreign languages ...'

In the hopes of improving her language teaching methodology, Han Nah began a teaching English to speakers of other languages (TESOL) certificate program in 2003 at Atlantic University. She undertook a specific program, designed for students who wanted to complete introductory courses in the field of TESOL, but did not want to complete a master's program or obtain K–12 certification. For Han Nah, a certificate program was ideal, since she had earned a master's degree in Korea. Under a certificate program requirement, she completed five courses, which allowed her to teach adults in both English as a second language (ESL) and EFL contexts. After entering this TESOL program, she came to the realization that many Korean students entered into TESOL programs in order to 'learn English.

Through TESOL, not just the way of teaching, learn English through the program, which [was] the first goal' (Interview, 1/6). As for Han Nah, she came into a TESOL program with an additional agenda for herself: 'I [did not] come into TESOL to learn how to teach English, but how to teach foreign languages to people who do not speak that language. It is really helpful for me because I already know foreign languages other than English' (Interview, 1/4). Han Nah's interest in learning about effective foreign language teaching methodology led her to gain admission into a TESOL certification program housed in Atlantic University.

'[Korean society] is a good society for men [and native speakers of English] ...': Expanding her Professional Identity in the US

Although Han Nah would love to remain in the US with her family, she said that if her husband were to get a better opportunity in Korea, they would have to move back to Korea. 'It is a good society for men, even though the man is lower level than women in terms of educational credentials, he can become more successful in his life than women [in Korea]' (Interview, 2/8). Reflecting on that imagined future, Han Nah did not know whether she could work in Korea, for she believed that there would be many obstacles for a married woman in her mid-thirties such as herself. On the other hand, she could envision herself teaching children, but even with that, her concern was that 'it would be very hard for me to work at a private English institute, because they want very young and more, very competitive to get into institute, since they have high salary' (Interview, 2/8). She did think about what her imagined future would be, teaching in Korea, if given that opportunity. She envisioned herself teaching English grammar, reading or listening. 'Although I have been learning much useful method for communicative lesson in English class, I may not have any chance to teach English in the way I have learned it' (E-Reflective Q/A, 11/25). Due to the dominant educational system in Korea and the practice of teaching to college entrance examinations, Korean public schools and some language institutes wanted teachers to teach more grammar in order to prepare students for those examinations. The social and educational norm in Korea was that native-English-speaking teachers were ideal for teaching speaking and communication skills.

According to Han Nah, her future in Korea would not be promising. Han Nah stated that 'it is a good society for men, even though man is lower level than woman in terms of educational credentials, he can become more successful in his life than women [in Korea]' (Interview, 2/8). Her future prospects of working as a professional in the Korean educational context were gloomy. She indicated that she would probably resort to teaching

English, since teaching Korean would only be available for graduates of teachers' colleges in Korea. In thinking about her pedagogy as an English language instructor within the Korean educational context, she indicated that she probably would not be able to provide English instruction in the way that it should be provided in Korea or elsewhere, due to national mandates on the college entrance examinations. Unless the Ministry of Education restructured the contents of the college entrance examinations in Korea, Han Nah and other English teachers in Korea would be dictated by the requirements for the college entrance examinations.

Han Nah's expansion of her professional identities would grow more strongly were the family to continue to live in the US. With this in mind, she indicated her trepidation about returning to Korea with regard to her professional and gendered identities. Returning to Korea, in large part, would represent limitations on possibilities for Han Nah as a woman, as a professional and as a mother raising two children in the Korean educational contexts. It would be a step down in every aspect of her life were they to return to Korea, given that her ideas with respect to educational improvement and the professional identities of women would be checked by dominant images of society, namely men in higher places.

'After you get married, you never compare with someone who never gets married and just study'

As Han Nah was thinking back to her gendered experience within her home and school in Korea, she remembered her mother's words. Her mother told Han Nah and her sisters to be successful in their academic pursuits during high school, but seek a different pathway shortly thereafter: '[A]fter finish[ing] college, you have to get married with someone who is very successful' (Interview, 2/1). In some respects, Han Nah agreed with her mother:

> In Korea, it is really hard for women to have success in their family and success in their life career. So she just focused on family first, because she always thinks that someone who has career [could] never get married. Someone who get married [would be] without career. (Interview, 2/1)

Han Nah discussed navigating the balancing act of her work and her family through 10 years (1995–2005) of experience as a married woman. She established lower expectations for herself, and did not believe in being a perfectionist. More importantly, she decided not to compare herself to single women with careers. With this philosophy, she noted that it was possible for her to be a career woman and a mother/spouse and do them well. Reflecting on her own experience, Han Nah gave me some advice about my roles as both a married woman and a professional woman:

> You may feel that after you get married, you may not be successful that much in your studies. After you get married, you never compare with someone who never gets married and just study. You can find a woman who can work for you. [Your] mother [can] take care of your child, and your housework; then you can work outside and you can maybe work inside and outside. (Interview, 2/15)

Han Nah realized that finding someone to help her with her household chores was harder than she had imagined, but she believed that it would be the best option for a woman such as herself to navigate her career life and her family life. Han Nah's rule of thumb has been to be content with herself and her husband and the multiplicity of roles established for her by the societies in Korea and the US.

Throughout interacting with Han Nah as well as her narratives constructed by me, I came to reflect more deeply about my lived/living history. The disclosing of my biography and my struggles in wrestling with the issues of language, gender and race inherent in my experiences navigating through both Korean and Western educational contexts led to my utilization of Denzin's (1989) concept of feminist, communitarian ethical framework, which entailed striving to build collaborative, reciprocal, trusting and friendly relations with Han Nah. Just as the construct of gender was a determining, complex, contradictory and fluid entity in Han Nah's lived experiences, my gendered identity has shaped my roles as daughter, spouse, teacher educator and mother in academia. From another methodological standpoint, I can confidently state that our dancing around each others' identity positions and providing each other with ways to make the most out of our shaped and yet-to-be-shaped identities resulted in more in-depth conversations and powerful understanding of each other's identities. By weaving my own story and experiences throughout my interviews with Han Nah, I became a 'real, history[ical] individual with concrete, specific desires and interests and not an invisible, anonymous voice of authority' (Harding, 1987: 9). All in all, this interpretive dance process was echoed by Toma (2000: 182), who stated, 'because subjective qualitative research is inherently personal, researchers cannot and should not hide their attachment to the topic and the persons that they study. The attachment is what makes the two way data collection process work'.

The dialogic inquiry engaged in with Han Nah was a liberating and educational experience for me. I learned through her life history, and I am more cognizant of how gendered norms influence my teacher and professional identities. I came to realize that the gendered experiences of Han Nah as a married woman became powerful images in renegotiating her identities within the US and Turkish contexts. The assigned identity of wife placed her in the situation of having to put aside or alter her career goals to be with her husband, and resulted in her experiencing a double consciousness. Specifically, for Han Nah, the double consciousness meant living in between tensions created by her desire to obtain a higher education degree in contexts other than her home country and her husband's career paths, as well as other familial obligations. Moreover, tensions between her Korean cultural norms and her desire to be an independent woman scholar surfaced. For Han Nah, getting married, moving to the US and having children changed her life and career trajectory from what she had envisioned for herself earlier in her educational journey. Being married and having children pushed her into having to construct and negotiate her imagined future identities as a professional Korean woman, a spouse and a mother. In her roles as a wife and mother, Han Nah needed to think about and balance the best possible future options for both her husband and her children. This included having to make sacrifices with respect to her own career aspirations to accommodate her husband, whose international position could move them elsewhere in the future. In this regard, Han Nah's experiences contradicted what she wanted to experience as a professional woman. This contradiction paralleled Sandra Harding's (1987: 7) statement: 'Not only do our gender experiences vary across the cultural categories; they also are often in conflict in any one individual's experience' .

Notes

(1) With the *Journal of Language Identity and Education* editors' permission, sections of this chapter come from Park (2009).
(2) Spouses of international graduate students were not allowed to enter a degree program, nor have a paid job, post the 9/11 terrorist attack. As a result, Han Nah was not able to enter a degree program (except to take courses as a non-matriculated student), and she was not able to have a paying job during her husband's residency in a master's degree program in Finance.

5 Where Privilege Meets Marginalization in the Narratives of Liu, Xia and Yu Ri: Exploring Their Linguistic and Teacher Identities[1]

The longer I stay here, the stronger I feel being excluded by the culture. (Liu, E-Journal, 12/15)

The fact that mentor teacher cares for EVERYONE [her emphasis] regardless of your background is more than admirable. (Liu, Interview, 4/27)

Not only in the program but the whole environment makes me feel so powerless because I think language is power. I don't have strong language capability so I feel powerless myself. Inside of me, I feel powerless. The fact is that I am powerless because [I] am just a traveler or an immigrant. (Xia, Interview, 12/27)

I am never afraid of being recognized as an NNES. I am kind of proud of that way. I speak English and they understand me. They can recognize that it is not my first language. I speak two languages. I always think that way and I am very positive. (Xia, Interview, 1/10)

I feel more comfortable to take the class [with other Asian women] because I can ask questions, if I did not understand the questions from the professors. (Yu Ri, Interview, 12/27)

[A] good experience to get up early in the morning. I felt that students [in her student teaching] were more open to me due to my NNES status. (Yu Ri, Interview, 3/2)

The above excerpts illuminate the experiences each woman had while being matriculated in their US teaching English to speakers of other languages (TESOL) programs. In particular, within each woman's paired excerpts, there is a glimpse of the transformation that occurred, going from taking courses in the program to being in classrooms as student teachers. The transformation that occurred for each woman, while very different for each, is the focus of this chapter, as I share the narrative snapshots of Liu, Xia and Yu Ri. While the above excerpts only focus on going from participating in TESOL program courses to being student teachers in US public school classrooms, in this chapter, I share each woman's narrative snapshots that depict their engagement with English in their home countries, their experiences working for professional companies, their experiences leading up to and being matriculated in US TESOL programs and their engagement with mentor teachers and students in (pre)student teaching experiences.

For the most part, the three women's experiences can be defined within the framework of privileged backgrounds. This was initiated by being introduced to English at early ages through the public educational systems in their native countries, private language institutes and/or early study abroad programs. Xia and Yu Ri's experience in their study abroad programs, Liu's work experience in the international company and all three women obtaining master's degrees in the US were additional forms of privilege afforded to them, which were emblematic of social and cultural capital. Nevertheless, they faced tensions and conflicts that were deeply embedded in their relationships to the English language. Having access to English language learning and teaching communities also brought forth much distress and frustrations, because the women could not equate themselves with native English speakers (NESs) when it came to English language fluency, pronunciation and academic discourse (Flowerdew, 1999, 2000). Within these communities, they saw themselves as always having to question their legitimacy vis-à-vis the English language.

This dominant theme of their linguistic identities influencing their teacher identities, and vice versa, was prevalent in the narrative accounts of Liu, Xia and Yu Ri. They identified themselves as international nonnative English speakers (NNESs) 'who have earned their undergraduate degrees [partly in the case of Yu Ri] in home countries where English was not the [primary] language of instruction' (Brady & Gulikers, 2004: 207). It was through their participation within these learning and teaching communities that they began to understand their identities in connection with the English language, their native languages and their East Asian heritage. Furthermore, it was within these communities of practice that their situated learning occurred, their NNES visibility became more apparent and they began to think about their future imagined possibilities as multilinguals (Amin, 2004; Cook, 1999; Lave & Wenger, 1991; Norton, 2000; Wenger, 1998).

This chapter aims to highlight the three women's linguistic and teacher identities, and how these identities shifted from their native countries to the US TESOL programs and, ultimately, to their newly established teaching contexts. In this sense, for Liu, Xia and Yu Ri, being privileged came with a sense of marginalization that coexisted in their experiences as burgeoning TESOL professionals.

Linguistic Experiences During Early Years: Sense of (Dis)Empowerment

Liu, Xia and Yu Ri felt pressured by the competition and the compulsory testing requirements that were embedded in the public educational systems in their native countries. Nevertheless, they continued to push forward with their English language learning in the midst of this pressure and competition. In the early years, learning English in their native countries, each woman had a particular pull that enabled her to enjoy the English language. Liu saw the 'magic' that came with learning English. For Xia, it was the weekend enrichment program she attended from elementary through high school that really started her on the road to equating herself as a legitimate English speaker. This was due to having been introduced to using English authentically and also having been exposed to NESs as teachers. For Yu Ri, it was both an English teacher in Korea and her one-year study abroad in New York that sparked her interest in enhancing her English language abilities.

English as 'full of magic!'

Since Liu's first encounter with English in middle school in China at the age of 12, '[learning English has become] something full of magic that holds me to it till today. I never stop learning it ever since then' (Liu, E-Journal, 11/25). She worked hard, getting up at 5 o'clock in the morning to listen to US radio broadcasts in order to hear the native English-speaking voices. She also read literature to become familiar with writing conventions. There were times when she felt frustrated in terms of not knowing the historical and cultural background of the discussion topic. But 'you never feel you learn the language completely, which makes me keep going and studying. This full of magic was all about learning different phrases to say the same things, expressing the same ideas in different ways, and want[ing] to be a part of that. Even though most of my experience was about memorizing, retelling and taking the multiple-choice tests, I still benefit[ted] a lot from this way of learning' (E-Journal, 11/25). Liu's experience learning English in China became a strong foundation for her educational journey in the US.

'I benefitted more from weekend enrichment program ...'

Although Xia excelled in her studies in the Chinese public schools, she did not like memorizing vocabulary words or translating English to Chinese, and vice versa. Although some English classes were supplemented with technology-aided lessons, she thought that they were boring and redundant, due to the 'misuse of the technology. It's like moving the whole textbook onto the website or onto the disk' (Xia, Interview, 12/27). Then she began the weekend enrichment classes as a fourth grader:

> I benefited more from [the] weekend 'enrichment' schools [where] the English class is more interactive and the teacher speaks better English. [They] will find pen pal in other countries for us to write with and pair us as chatting partners. Also [I] had native-English-speaking guest teachers from time to time. (E-Journal, 10/17)

Xia attended the weekend enrichment English program until she graduated from high school in 1997. She was amazed by the fact that her teachers pushed students to use English as a tool for communication; hence, she was immersed in an English-speaking environment. For instance, the pen pal experience, via the weekend program project, provided Xia with the desire and motivation to have a better grasp of the English language for communication purposes.

While she enjoyed learning English in the weekend enrichment English program, she stated that her high school years (1994–1997), preparing for the college entrance examination, were gloomy due to the nature of focusing on test-taking strategies.

> In my high school, the teacher did not even speak a full sentence in English. They just said a, b, c and d. Since it was a multiple choice, they focused on correct answers all the time. Every class, they [gave] us the right answers. They [would] explain the answers in Chinese. (Xia, Interview, 12/27)

Xia perfected her test-taking strategies and became very confident in her ability to excel in every subject related to the English language, since the goal was to do well on school and national exams. 'English [was] never a difficult subject to me, especially at school, where the main purpose of English teaching [was] passing exams' (Interview, 12/27). Although she excelled academically, she realized the limitations that the Chinese public educational system had placed on her being able to teach English.

'[Use] English as a communication tool ...'

Yu Ri's one-year stay in New York at the age of 13 started out as a scholarly endeavor for her father, who was a visiting scholar at a university during the 1992–1993 academic year. For Yu Ri, staying in New York with her family as a middle-school student brought forth complexities, both as a middle-school student needing to return to her academic work load in Korea after one year and as an English language learner in the US. As a result, during her one-year stay in the US, she worked with her mother, reviewing and catching up with math and Korean classes, using textbooks that her mother brought from Korea. 'I had to study Korean subjects in the United States. I can remember that [it] was stressful, that I should not be far behind compared to other students who were studying in Korea since I was scheduled to return in one year' (Yu Ri, Interview, 1/26). In New York, her sources of stress, in addition to having to study Korean subjects as well as the American school subjects, were that she never experienced the language problem in Korea and she felt like an outsider in the American classroom settings.

Upon returning to Korea in 1993, Yu Ri came to the realization that she wanted to learn English as a way of communication. She knew this was difficult to do in Korea because there were not that many English speakers. She saw herself 'talking to herself in English' (Yu Ri, Interview, 1/26). She focused on activities like listening to music and the radio, and watching TV. However, more often than not, learning English in middle school in Korea was textbook driven and focused on reading and listening, the kind of teaching, she thought, that made students in the classroom passive, bored and dysfunctional when talking with English-speaking foreigners in Korea.

Yu Ri, too, realized that there was no way to get away from the pressure of entrance exams, since it was one of the most important parts, if not the most important part, of her Korean high-school life. Even through this mundane preparation for the college entrance exam, Yu Ri sought out ways to improve her conversational English skills. She was influenced by native-English-speaking teachers, due to the manner in which they taught conversational English classes. 'It was teachings [that led to] use English as a communication tool' (Yu Ri, Interview, 1/26). Furthermore, a specific middle-school English teacher had greatly influenced her through her duties as a 'young-uh-boo-jahng ['class leader' in Korean]. We were kind of close, and she gave me newspapers, cartoons and English books, and I really appreciated her' (Yu Ri, Interview, 2/23). Even though she felt that she was not successful in adjusting to the educational system in New York, Yu Ri's experience in New York during her middle-school years became a fuel that ignited her desire to learn the English language as a communication tool throughout the continuation of her studies in Korea and beyond.

Professional Experiences in their Native Countries

For all three women, their professional experience (teaching, interning, choosing college major) in their home countries triggered them to re-envision their future educational and professional goals. Liu's teaching

English in China and working for a company in Beijing became the fuel for her to leave China for the US. Xia's interning at a book publishing company in China, as well as her majoring in European Studies in Germany, pushed her into the US. As for Yu Ri, her one-year study in New York, as well as her college educational experience in Korea at a second-tier university, caused her to continue to question her status as a college student in Korea.

'When you teach English, you are changing someone's life ...'

Although Liu's strong sense of linguistic and racial identities as a multilingual were omnipresent throughout her early educational and work experiences, her linguistic identity was challenged in later years as a tutor in China. During her college years in China, from 1996 to 2000, she home-tutored a high school student to help him organize what he needed to memorize and understand via a variety of strategies in preparation for his college entrance examination. She felt that through her tutoring experience, she had the responsibility to change another person's life.

> When you teach English, you are changing someone's life, and that is such a burden. You did not want someone's life to be hanging on your shoulders. But sometimes I feel a lot of pressure when thinking a person's life is under your control; therefore, I chose to teach business English. (Liu, Interview, 2/1)

While some would feel that tutoring students and helping them navigate their learning trajectory could be perceived as an act of accomplishment, Liu realized that tutoring the high school student became more work emotionally than she was able to handle. She knew that she loved teaching English, but felt that she should find a different venue, where she and the student could both learn as a way to improve the quality of their lives. Since business administration was her college major, Liu began teaching business English in 1999 in small groups as well as in company classes, after completing two years of tutoring the high school student.

Through this business-English teaching experience, she realized that she liked talking to people not only about their business ventures, but also about strategies for improving their English as businessmen and businesswomen. Teaching business English gave her comfort, 'even though we both have [an] accent and made some mistakes' (E-Journal, 11/25). Her role as a business-English teacher gave her opportunities to know different people, bring new knowledge to them and open a window to their worlds.

'I wanted to find a good chance in Beijing ...'

Because Liu majored in business administration and English literature in a college located near Beijing, she saw her interest to be in international business. At that point, she stated, 'I am going to be a business woman dealing with international [related matters] in the future' (Liu, Interview, 3/16). Liu landed a job in an international trading operation, but she did not envision any growth and development for herself as a businesswoman working in her hometown of Datong, and wanted to find opportunities in Beijing, a center of international business growth and development. As a result, Liu turned down the job offer in Datong, taking an offer in Beijing that had very little connection to international business ventures.

> I did not want to go back to my hometown. I wanted to find a good chance in Beijing and I did, but it was not what I really wanted to do. But it helped me to stay in Beijing. It had nothing to do with international business. I felt sad for a long time about this, because that is not what I expected for the rest of my life. (Liu, Interview, 3/16)

Liu also commented that even though working for the Beijing company was not where her heart was, she 'got used to it' (Interview, 3/16). It meant envisioning a bigger world for herself by working in Beijing, as opposed to a small town like Datong.

In order to continue her vision of this 'bigger world', Liu sought out graduate degree programs in the US around her college completion time in 2000. According to Liu, most Chinese people went to Australia, Ireland or England to study because of the low exchange rate, lower tuition and the availability of work in places such as supermarkets, where international students could legally earn spending money. Liu's reasons for coming to the US as opposed to other English-speaking countries were that only the universities in US offered fellowships and scholarships for Chinese master's-level students and that they also ranked higher in overseas education among the schools in English-speaking countries. She stated, 'Nothing could be more attractive than achieving master's degree in education and be around an English-speaking environment in the United States' (Liu, E-Journal, 11/25).

'Don't invest too much time or energy!'

Xia entered college as an English literature major in 1997. While she was in college, she interned at a publishing company, where the focus was on developing technology-aided English textbooks. She believed that the role of publishing companies was to cater to the needs of English teachers in both the public and private education sectors. As an editor on the design team, she worked closely with a technology specialist, developing an online English language textbook and programs. Xia and her design team colleagues developed a text for the English book, and the technology specialist's role was to transfer this into appropriate online text. Xia felt that the innovative ideas of her design team were often hampered due to her boss's need to speed things up. 'Don't invest too much time or energy, and just do what the textbook does. Something innovative, he said no, but something identical to the textbook he would say yes' (Xia, Interview, 12/27). After working at this company for several years, she realized that her innovative ideas to bring forth technology-aided English language learning programs had barriers that she could not overcome.

'[It] really was not a test. It's like a talk ...'

While working at the publishing company in China, she felt the need to experience a different educational context. Her boyfriend at that time was planning to go abroad to study, so Xia researched some schools in the US and Germany. They applied to programs in both the US and Germany; however, her boyfriend was admitted into an engineering program in Germany and not in the US. Xia, on the other hand, was admitted into a TESOL program in the US and a European studies program in Germany. After much consideration, she decided to be with her boyfriend and deferred her TESOL program admission in the US for one year to embark on a different program in Germany in 2002. This MA program was in European studies, encompassing politics, economics, history and law, as well as an organized overview of Europe and its history. During her time in Germany, she experienced language knowledge construction and production that she had never experienced in China. All of the weekly exams in her program were administered orally in German.

> I appreciated the assessment system in Germany because it really was not a test. It's like a talk. Professors really want to know how much you know. It's also very good opportunity for students if they have questions. They can ask questions and it's very interactive. I like that. [But], it's probably too hard for me. (Xia, Interview, 2/3)

She gave up this program after one year and left her boyfriend in Germany to embark on the US TESOL program in 2003.

'[Yeo Ja] University was not regarded as a good school in Korea'

Although Yu Ri thought about possibly attending a co-educational high school, she gave in to her mother's alumna connection and recommendation to enter a foreign language high school in 1996. This school was highly regarded in the Korean educational system and teachers were very liberal, such that physical abuse from the teachers was uncommon, unlike other high schools in the Korean educational system. This school had a mandatory after-school study period, during which everyone gathered in one classroom to study and practice test-taking and basic skills from 17:30–21:00 every evening until the college entrance exam time. This lasted for three years.

However, Yu Ri began to experience a different learning situation in some of her Korean high school classes, interacting with native-English-speaking teachers as instructors in conversation classes twice a week. Students in these conversation classes were given English names and learned about American customs and cultures. She realized that taking conversational classes with an NES teacher in high school gave her confidence in speaking English. At this school, Yu Ri met a teacher who showed that she cared for her students, remembered all the students' names, encouraged students to ask questions and also invited her students to her home during holidays.

Yu Ri was disappointed at her college entrance exam scores, and had to settle on entering Yeo Ja University in 1999. In 2001, Yu Ri transferred to Atlantic University with junior-year status in the international relations department, for several reasons. First, she desired to learn more about the academic discourse in the US for which she had been initially introduced as a middle-school student in New York back in 1992. She felt that she had not adapted to the learning environment as a middle-school student in New York; therefore, she sought out another opportunity to study in the US. 'I wanted to try to adapt to the American culture [for the second time] because I did not adapt well before [in middle school in N.Y.]. I wanted to know how I [could] survive in the American educational system' (Yu Ri, Interview, 1/26). The second reason for transferring to the US was that she perceived herself to be a failure, since she had not been able to enter one of the leading women's universities in Korea. In that respect, she stated:

> I was not quite satisfied with myself because I did not like [Yeo Ja University] when I first got into that university because I had graduated from a foreign-language high school, where all the smart and intelligent people attended, but [Yeo Ja University] was not regarded as a good school [in Korea]. So I was kind of disappointed at myself because I was not that good. I needed to compensate through coming here and study. (Yu Ri, Interview, 1/31)

English Language Identity: Coexistence of Privilege and Marginalization in Being (Dis)Empowered

All three women were influenced by the English language during their early years, which had a lasting impression on their future educational and professional endeavors.

Liu's identity as a multilingual was strong throughout her educational journey in China because of her high academic achievement. Liu seemed very confident in her abilities, and felt that there was nothing that could slow her down in terms of learning English and what she wanted to do with the language later in life. This sense of confidence could have been related to how she viewed the English language as being 'full of magic'. Even though both Liu and Xia were products of the same educational system in China, their experiences with the public school education differed. Xia recognized the fact that the Chinese public school system had limited her in terms of learning the English language, since the Chinese English curricula had not enabled her to expand her oral communication skills. It simply helped her to expand her test-taking strategies, in that learning English in high school was synonymous with learning strategies to score high on exams. Similarly, Yu Ri was disenchanted with the Korean educational system, with its slavish adherence to rote memorization and regurgitation of information involving the English language to pass the exams. This was similar to what Xia had recounted. When Yu Ri came to New York during her middle school years, she re-evaluated her learning goals with respect to the English language. When she realized that she could learn English, primarily for the purpose of communication, she began to refocus her vision for herself in relation to learning English. Even with this realization, Yu Ri's one-year stay in New York was not without challenges, because she had not been taught how to navigate the US academic classroom discourse, and the fact that she still had to study subjects in the Korean educational curriculum for her impending return to Korea.

Overall, all three women's early educational contexts provided them with strong foundations in learning and using English, which led them to other opportunities within and beyond their home countries.

Challenging Experiences in the US: Language, Culture and Power

It was evident that the linguistic identities of Liu, Xia and Yu Ri were transformed once they came to the English-speaking countries, due to a host of problems related to how English was perceived in the worldwide context and who was seen as legitimate owners and users of English (Amin, 2004; Widdowson, 1994). Specifically, all three women began to compare themselves to NESs in their classes. They began to question all they had accomplished back in their native countries with respect to learning and using English, which they could not put into appropriate communicative applications in the US. This was ironic, as all three had gained entrance into the US educational system (Liu and Xia in TESOL and Yu Ri transferring into undergraduate studies before her TESOL program) due to their excellent command of the English language in their native countries. All three women began to identify their 'self-perceived language needs as well as self-perceived prejudices' as they interacted with NESs and some immigrant NNESs in different communities (Kamhi-Stein *et al.*, 2004: 83). In particular, their linguistic identities encompassed how they positioned themselves and how the dominant culture, as well as their local cultures, positioned them in relation to the English language (Pasternak & Bailey, 2004; Varghese et al., 2005). There were many situations in which Liu, Xia and Yu Ri felt powerless and uncomfortable related to their production of the English language. Liu stated that she felt like an outsider vis-à-vis her classmates, who dominated the classroom conversations. Xia indicated strong feelings of powerlessness, most notably with respect to her linguistic and racial identity. She provided an example of these feelings of powerlessness by noting that she was a traveler and an immigrant. With regard to Yu Ri, she made a comment at one point in which she described always being uncomfortable participating in class.

'The longer I stay, the stronger I feel being excluded ...'

In reflecting on her experience in some TESOL program courses, Liu felt that she was just 'sitting [in classrooms] listening, not really participating in the discussion'. She stated that she learned a lot by just listening, and she also commented that '[n]o participation [did] not mean [she was] not learning' (Liu, Interview, 2/15). She felt that 'participation' should come in different forms in order to reach out to different learning styles. In Liu's experience, native speakers in her classes liked to talk, and 'the native [English-speaking] students would give some points that would broaden my horizon, but I don't think sometimes they make good points' (Interview, 2/28). Liu's experience was that some NNESs would like to vocally participate in class discussion, but that they did not really have much time, and most of the discussion time was 'taken up by the native speakers, so we [just kept] silent. We only do group discussions and group studies, and international students are grouped to study together because we can understand each other better' (Interview, 2/28). She realized that there were other ways for her to participate in the class.

When she did participate in other forms, other issues surfaced. One classmate stated that Liu's English was good enough, and that she might just be too fussy about her English language proficiency, in that she was too focused on her speech, rather than the meaning. Liu's perspective on this discussion led her to think that perhaps the NESs with whom she had interacted in her TESOL program expected Asian students to be silent in class, such that Asian students were already seen as others in their (NES) minds. 'When they say that my English is good enough, I understand they are trying to be nice, but it actually hurt a lot if it is not the fact' (E-Journal, 12/15). The comment that Liu's English was 'good enough' bothered her, because she always thought that her English was NOT (her stress) good enough. She believed that it may have been good enough for communication and expressing her ideas, but not good enough to function on the academic level. Her expectations for herself have always been high. 'So if they said

[English is good enough] to me many times, I feel it is not true.' Liu wanted to know their real opinion, not just 'good' said in the interest of being nice. 'I don't know other people, but my personality will always tell me to tell the truth to other souls' (Interview, 2/28). Before coming to the US, she was proud of her English language abilities, and now she felt it to be a deficit and even an obstacle. 'The longer I stay here, the stronger I feel being excluded by the culture' (E-Journal, 12/15).

'... the whole environment makes me feel powerless ...'

Xia had gained admission into several TESOL programs in the US, but decided to enter the Pacific University TESOL program, because '[the people in this metropolitan area were] better and well educated' (Interview, 2/8). She definitely did not want to be in a country where people could 'purchase' degrees. 'You study one year [in England] and get a master's, and they go back to China, and just can't find a job because people know that a degree from England means nothing' (Interview, 2/8). Her belief was that she needed to be in an environment where people were better educated, which meant that she could have more opportunities to construct her experience and knowledge.

Xia's expectations from her TESOL program were crystal clear. She wanted to do research with a professor, but she was not allowed initially, due to her master's-level status:

> In my personal statement, I stated what I wanted to do in my master's program. But when I came here, it's not exactly what it turned out to be. [M]y advisor was not very supportive about me doing research. She simply stated that master's students were not expected to do research. I talked with her about that, but she did not respond at all. (Interview, 12/27)

After this rejection, Xia emailed another professor in the program, Dr Jennings, who welcomed her into one of her research projects. Before she commenced conducting research with Dr Jennings, Xia felt restless just taking classes. 'I felt really bored because there [was] no new things coming into my mind, repeating what I have learned before. I just wanted to do something outside of class but there was just no chance to do them' (Interview, 12/27). Xia wanted to go beyond taking courses, as she wanted to experience this culture and know the educational system in the US, in order to improve the educational system in China. Xia desired to enrich her own knowledge and experience, but also wanted to change the lives of people by bringing new ways of learning and teaching back to China. Xia yearned for an enriching experience in her master's program, and later in her PhD program. She wanted to become a scholar and teacher. 'I have never been satisfied by [just taking courses.] I think the degree does not really mean a lot to me at certain point. It is what you really get from here. It's what [I] have in mind. I can even buy a degree from England. I am looking for experience' (Interview, 12/27). To Xia, an enriching experience meant going beyond taking courses instituted in her program requirement. She was at Pacific University to gain a different kind of learning experience compared to what she had gained in China. She wanted to do more critical thinking in her overall educational journey in the US.

From the beginning of her master's TESOL program in the US, she had felt powerless even though some of her professors and colleagues nurtured her educational journey.

> Not only in the program but the whole environment makes me feel so powerless because I think language is power. I don't have strong language capability so I feel powerless myself. Inside of me, I feel powerless. The fact is that I am powerless because [I] am just a traveler or an immigrant. (Interview, 12/27)

For Xia, being proficient in the English language meant wielding power in different situations. But as an NNES who was not quite proficient in the English language, she perceived herself to have a lower status in her TESOL program. She constantly needed to interact with NESs, since she was not sure that people truly comprehended her. The fact that people either repeated what Xia said, or figured out what she said by emitting non-verbal cues, was evidence to her that she held incomprehensible communicative skills.

'I feel more comfortable to take the class with [other Asian women] …'

Yu Ri became interested in TESOL during her undergraduate years in Korea for a multitude of reasons. These included the experience that she had gleaned from her high school education, as well as the influences that different English conversation teachers had imparted on her, contributing to her desire to learn more about the linguistic structure of the language. Furthermore, since her university in Korea did not offer TESOL as an undergraduate major, but did offer it for master's students, she opted to come to the US to finish her undergraduate degree prior to gaining admission into a MATESOL program in the US. She wanted to learn the language so that she could also learn the cultural and practical aspects of English. She viewed being in the TESOL program as getting one step closer to becoming a TESOL professional.

In terms of classroom interactions, Yu Ri stated, 'I feel more comfortable to take the class [with other Asian women] because I can ask questions, if

I did not understand the questions from the professors' (Interview, 1/17). Her explanation for this was that being with other students who were like her racially and linguistically, prevented her from having to masquerade as an NES, which she would have felt compelled to do if she were the only NNES in the program. As an NNES student in a US classroom, many different types of participation in courses convinced her that she was communicating effectively with professors through more than simply whole-class discussions. Professors could see that she had more to contribute through different means than just oral participation in class.

For Yu Ri, because she could not engage herself in whole-class discussion, unlike her NES classmates, she engaged more actively in online discussions, written assignments and group projects, which were all part of the course requirements. Yu Ri stated that, due to the availability of multiple means with which to participate in graduate TESOL courses, she felt that she was given opportunities to interact with her professors.

> If the class has many kinds of activities, like small groups or journals [online], or quizzes, then I feel like I am communicating more to the professors or the classmates. If the class offers one type of activity, then I feel like not learn much or I don't communicate with the professors in the class. (Interview, 1/17)

This, in fact, enabled her professors to assess Yu Ri and others through the students' use of other means to contribute to the knowledge base of the class. This was also echoed in Hawkins' (2004) and Kamhi-Stein's (2000) discussions of how students who were perceived to be silent in class became more vocal and participatory in the online discussions. Moreover, Jewell (2003: 57) confirms that 'students have been shown to contribute more and at higher levels of linguistic complexity; to computer-mediated communication than in face-to-face situations'.

Furthermore, her professors who came from diverse backgrounds also encouraged her own journey as an NNES. 'I can be more motivated because [this one teacher] speaks English fluently. I [am] impressed' (Interview, 1/31). For Yu Ri, this particular professor was a role model in that she could also overcome linguistic and cultural barriers in order to teach English. In discussing the professors who had the most positive impact on her education, she cited as the best the professors who brought in hands-on material, allowed for participation and provided work in small groups, which was less intimidating than speaking in front of the entire class. She also appreciated professors who gave clear and succinct examples to illustrate theory in practice in TESOL courses. One particular professor that Yu Ri was fond of was not only knowledgeable and organized in her teaching, but she also provided different forms of learning activities in her courses.

Seeking Out Professional Opportunities as Graduate Assistants

Both Liu and Xia were offered graduate assistantships as part of their master's in TESOL at the Pacific University, which was not the case for Yu Ri, being matriculated at the Atlantic University. While these assistantships provided much privilege and capital for both Liu and Xia, the issues of marginalization were inevitable for a host of reasons.

'No, I don't think so!'

In her role as a TESOL program assistant, Liu worked with a professor and a doctoral student on a project that had started before Liu joined her master's in TESOL program. On one particular day, they were working on a data set and Liu tried to explain to these two people why the data that they had collected was incorrect. 'Because I just got to the United States a few months ago, I tried to make my idea clear to them with my limited oral language proficiency. But they did not believe me and kept saying, "No, I don't think so"' (Interview, 2/28). Liu said that she continued to give a detailed explanation about the computation process, while they continued to insist that Liu's explanation was incorrect and did not listen to her. 'I can do nothing but wait for what results they got from their discussion, and they never confronted on the fact that my explanation was correct. I felt the situation had to do with [my status as a NNES]' (Interview, 2/28). Liu felt that the professor and the doctoral student ignored her explanation because they could not understand her English, and instead of trying to understand her and help Liu clarify her explanation, they disregarded her contribution to the program project.

'I told you so! It's kind of silence resists'

Liu had decided to stay quiet about the project results, even if she wanted to say, 'I told you so! It's kind of silence resists' (Interview, 2/28). She believed that arguing would make the relationship with them worse, 'so why not just keep silent. You can check all the files and you can find the mistakes by yourself and by that time, you are going to feel guilty for what you have done to me' (Interview, 3/18). Liu's thoughts on this event, coupled with her relegated role as a secretary instead of a respected contributor with valuable ideas, contributed to her attribution of the rejection of her ideas as being due to her perceived linguistic identity. This kind of experience reminded her of her racial identity as an East Asian woman working hard to 'tolerate and forgive people' in many different contexts. She strongly believed that the professor and the doctoral student would have treated her differently if she were an NES. 'I hope my voice could be heard in this so-called fair country' (E-Journal, 12/15). She positioned herself in the program as such: 'I have to just do my class work well, and get teachers impressed by my jobs in the class work, that's the only thing I can do' (Interview, 2/28).

Liu felt that international students were being looked down upon, and that native speakers had advantages since they were born into the English language, which gave them certain status in the TESOL program. Liu stated, 'Except for the academic knowledge, [I] still [had] great gap between other speakers. NES, speak English fluently. Even if I [knew] the academic knowledge well, [I] still [felt] less of a status because of language' (Interview, 2/28). Liu thought she needed to talk more in the classroom to convince 'myself and others even if I am not a native speaker, [that] I can still contribute something to the class, try to make friends with as many friends as possible, not only just Chinese friends. [If I do this, it can] make me feel kind of accepted in this environment, not isolate myself, push myself more within the community to be more participatory' (Interview, 2/28).

Reflecting on some of these negative experiences in her TESOL program made her realize how comfortable she had been in her native country in terms of interacting with different people. She stated that in most cases in China, people were always relying on her to get the right answer, and they listened to her instead of her listening to them. 'In all different contexts, people lean on me. They trust me and I am kind of a little bit above the capability of the average people. I am not saying that I am better than they are. In some aspect, I might be worth their trust. They listen to me, and accept my opinion' (Interview, 3/18). Liu's feelings of discomfort emanated from the fact that her feelings had been suppressed by people, language and culture.

> I think the language might be the major problem for me. Because at the beginning, I think when I catch up my language proficiency, everything is going on well and there will not be any problems. But it turned out to be different. You can't express ideas or share ideas with people. It just feels like you are alone. (Interview, 3/18)

Her level of comfort was very important to Liu, since she believed that her comfort level was related to her self-dignity. When she was not recognized, she became frustrated and upset with herself and others. During one of our interviews, I commented that her ideas were clear and she articulated her feelings well. To my comment, she responded, 'I have something to say. I have a lot of feelings inside of me' (Interview, 3/18).

'It's doing disservice to the students!'

An incident during her assistantship work at Pacific University exacerbated her sense of powerlessness about her identity, not only as an

NNES but also as a graduate student without any decision-making status. For several weeks during the fall 2004 semester, Xia worked with a professor and a doctoral student on state-mandated curriculum, also known as the National Standards System (NSS). She stated that her involvement in the NSS made her feel more powerless due to her student status, even though she worked day and night for several weeks to present the TESOL standards to the NSS supervisors. She could not make any suggestions to improve this politically mandated system.

> I have a lot to say about [NSS]. It's not practical. Each teacher has [her] own concerns about the students, not the standards. If the people who write the standards do not know how to teach the students, it [becomes disconnected]. It's not proper to their students. (Interview, 2/8)

After her experience with the NSS standards, Xia believed that the NSS could never satisfy the learning needs of multilingual children housed in the K–12 educational system, and that the NSS was just another way to wield control over the teachers of K–12 multilingual students.

Another incident during her professional development opportunity as a master's student brought forth a feeling of powerlessness. Xia felt that she not only had to prove her English language abilities to NESs, but that she had to prove her English language abilities to immigrant NNESs as well. When Xia was applying for an on-campus opportunity and realized that the contact person was Chinese, she decided to speak to her in Mandarin Chinese, so as to show linguistic collegiality. The Chinese woman contact erroneously concluded that because Xia was an international NNES student, that there was no way she would be able to understand the words and text written by other K–12 multilinguals, and stated: '[The students'] handwriting is very poor and their language is really poor, and you probably cannot read it because you are an NNES' (Interview, 1/25). After trying to explain to this recruiter that she herself was more than qualified for this temporary job, Xia was allowed to start if and only if she went through a training session, which was not stipulated in the original job requirement, '[to] see that whether I can score the test with validity or reliability, and if I pass the training session, then I can do the job' (Interview, 1/25).

The immigrant Chinese woman's statement did not make sense to Xia, and she believed that the test-scoring people wanted an NES who was also fluent in another language and not an international student. Her sense of powerlessness came with not being able to do anything about her identity as an NNES, even though this temporary test-scoring job asked for bilingual test scorers. She came to understand that this bilingual identity could never be legitimized if the person claimed a non-white race (Kubota & Lin, 2006).

Becoming an English Teacher: Emerging Sense of Multicompetent English Teacher Identities

Throughout privileged yet turbulent journeys, all three women gained much experience and knowledge navigating through their TESOL programs. The crux of their experiences and understanding about their teacher identities came with their volunteer teaching and (pre)student teaching experiences. I now turn to these experiences that shaped their teacher identities, which in many instances were in conflict with their identities as NNESs.

'The fact that mentor teacher cares for EVERYONE [emphasis original] ...'

During the spring of 2005, Liu observed some elementary and middle school classes and did one-on-one tutoring with some of the students in those classrooms, which was a prerequisite for her student teaching semester in fall 2005. During the spring 2005 semester, Liu started her pre-student teaching observation at a middle school, under the mentorship of a gifted teacher. He was from Africa, and had been in the US for over 20 years. He went through several schools to receive his bachelor's and master's degrees, and finally became a teacher. Liu was very impressed with the students because they responded to the teacher in an engaging way. Even though they were talkative and playful in the classroom, she saw that the mentor teacher and his students had good relationships in class. Liu strongly believed that a good relationship between teacher and students would motivate student learning. With this thought, Liu reflected on her role as a graduate student and some of her professors in relation to what she witnessed in the middle school with the mentor teacher and his students. She realized that she was not getting from her own program what the middle school students were getting from their mentor teacher. 'The fact that the mentor teacher cares for EVERYONE [her emphasis] [regardless of] your background is more than admirable. If they don't care too much about their own benefits, the students might feel better, and much to do with personality and experiences through the life' (Interview, 4/27). Liu also believed that certain kinds of experiences that her mentor teacher endured made him an effective teacher. She said that he had suffered a lot after he came to the US, and he understood what the students' parents were going through because he also went through that; as a result, he tried to assist his students both inside and outside of the class.

'I think the teachers play an important role [in motivating] students ...'

Sometimes, Liu wondered about what it would take for NNESs like herself to work as English teachers in the US. 'Sometimes, I feel [if] I would teach in this country, I might not be qualified because my language is not that good. How can I get on the platform and teach other students? How can I trust [myself] if I cannot speak [English] very well?' (Interview, 2/1). Liu believed that teachers needed to understand the students, their achievement levels and their difficulties, in order to be effective ESL teachers. Teachers must really love teaching, and know the responsibilities of their jobs.

> I think the teachers play an important role [in motivating] students. I like responsible teachers, careful about the future of the students. [As for teaching English in China,] most people who chose to teach either because they can't find a better job or because right now, the teachers get higher salary. Either money motivated or have no job availabilities. I think only small percentage of people really like to teach especially for young kids. (Interview, 3/16)

'It is impossible for [us] to speak native English, speak English as a native ...'

> He burst into laughter. He said that you were only here for one-and-a-half years and you are going to teach English? Foreign teachers who do not speak English well teach English to the kids who don't speak English. At the moment, I was kind of upset ... My English is not perfect, and how can I teach other people English? (Interview, 1/10)

This assessment prompted Xia to reveal her insecurities toward her English language proficiency: 'How could [I] teach other people English when [my] English was not perfect? It is impossible for [us] to speak native English, speak English as a native' (Interview, 1/10). Her ingrained belief was that if a person taught English, then she/he would have to be perfect in English; hence, one had to claim a native speaker of English identity in order to teach English. Xia began the first day of her student teaching experience in her master's degree TESOL program with an embarrassing incident. The first eight weeks of her student teaching were under the mentorship of an NNEST, Ms Tomiko (pseudonym). She was a native of Japan and had been teaching elementary ESL since 1999 upon completing her master's in TESOL program from a university in the mid-Atlantic region.

On the first day of her student teaching at Memory Lane Elementary School (pseudonym) located near Pacific University, Xia was nervous as she did not know what to expect from her students. She stated that her nervousness elevated in front of young children, and the situation exacerbated her anxiety when she had to communicate in English. After the first week of her student teaching, she articulated her understanding about the relationship between being a language teacher and levels of confidence. As a multilingual, Xia was confident about her English, since everyone could see that she was an NNES, and her language was 'good enough' to interact with both NNESs and NESs. However, her level of confidence altered when she shifted her role from a multilingual to an English as a second language (ESL) teacher. Xia stated, somewhat jokingly, that she could not use Chinglish (using English in a Chinese grammatical way, or codeswitching between Chinese and English) in the classroom, though it was perfectly fine to do so within the context of the graduate school program. Xia stated,

> But as a teacher, the situation is so different. It decreases my confidence. It's not like we can find excuses for ourselves in speaking Chinglish and sometimes having fun. I speak Chinglish purposefully having fun, but [I] can't do that as a teacher. (Interview, 1/10)

She wanted to be perfect in English in order to be seen as a good and credible teacher of ESL.

Xia viewed her identity as a TESOL graduate student to be different from her identity as an NNES ESL teacher. Xia's construction of identities as both a graduate student and an ESL teacher echoed Gee's (2004) construct of social languages. Gee posited that learning a language was equated to learning social languages within discourses. In other words, Xia's social languages would offer her ways not only to communicate informally with colleagues in her graduate school program, but also to be recognized by others as an English teacher using only proper English and not 'Chinglish' to teach ESL students. The very decision that Xia made about not using Chinglish in her ESL teaching setting is connected to the perceptions of what it means to be an ideal English teacher. Specifically, these pointed to the very nature of how English is perceived in the world. The dominant discourse upholding the notion that only NESs can teach ESL has been elaborately discussed and problematized by many scholars in the field of TESOL (Braine, 1999; Kamhi-Stein, 2004; Norton, 2000; Pavlenko & Blackledge, 2004; Widdowson, 1994).

Xia understood Ms Tomiko's pedagogy to be flawless, and her way of motivating and engaging her ESOL students came from her heart.

> [Ms Tomiko] is very professional and creative. She does a lot of hands-on in class, and she has so much emotional energy. She acts out a lot, and the kids just love her. She is a very good teacher; [The kids] can tell from your face, your eyes and they really like you. If you don't, then they can tell and they will stay away from you. They are like clams and they are going to close. (Interview, 1/25)

Xia felt that international people were under more pressure than the natives after observing Ms Tomiko's experience at the school and reflecting on her own experience as an international student. Xia could tell that her mentor teacher worked extremely hard in order to prove to herself and her mainstream teaching community that she was a credible teacher, and indeed qualified to teach ESL. Through working with and being mentored by Ms Tomiko, Xia came to better understand herself as an English for speakers of other languages (ESOL) practitioner, in that being an ESL teacher was more than knowing and delivering effective pedagogy; it was about caring for her multilingual students from all walks of life in the US. Even though Xia did not have a strong sense of identity as an ESL teacher, her sense of herself as an NNES was changing:

> I am never afraid of being recognized as an NNES. I am kind of proud of that way. I speak English and they understand me. They can recognize that it is not my first language. I speak two languages. I always think that way and I am very positive. I want to improve my English, but not for the purpose of being identified as a NES. (Interview, 1/10)

During her student teaching experience, she was observed by her university student teaching supervisor. Xia gained some valuable insight through listening to her supervisor's suggestions about classroom management, improving the delivery of lessons and being mindful of integrating state standards in the lesson plans. Although Xia understood her supervisor's comments and feedback on her lesson planning, she felt a disconnect between her own standards of pedagogy and the state-mandated standards. 'For me, I am kind of confused by the state standards and my own standards. [They] are so-called communicative teaching methods. It is so hard to carry out, especially when someone is sitting there and observing you' (Interview, 2/3). Xia wanted to carry out her communicative teaching methods, where her multilingual students viewed English as a tool for communication, within a step-by-step lesson plan. However, she also had to think and be mindful about the different objectives and types of activities mandated by the state standards and curriculum. Xia was compelled to continue making lesson plans that included the integration of standards and state mandates into her ESL curriculum, such that she did not think it would be possible to genuinely engage communicatively with her students in class.

'… [P]robably, I will show her what teaching is …'

The second placement during her student teaching semester was in a high school ESL classroom, with a mentor teacher very much different from Ms Tomiko. According to Xia, Ms Harley, an NES, was more interested in administration than in teaching. 'I know [Ms Tomiko] is exceptional. I did not expect that this second mentor teacher would be as good as she is, but at least, she should go through all the steps in giving a lesson. [I]t is not giving a lesson. Go back to your seat and do whatever you want' (Interview, 3/15). Xia felt that she was not given a clear set of directions on her roles and responsibilities as a student teacher. She could not put up with sitting for the entire day, so on the third day, she walked around the classroom and helped the students during their independent work. 'I can't bear [sitting at my desk]. I just walked around looking for something to do myself. She [was] fine with it' (Interview, 3/15).

However, Ms Harley did suggest an idea that Ms Tomiko had not, during the first eight weeks. Ms Harley wanted to interact with Xia through a dialogue journal, a venue for the two to communicate Xia's experiences. Xia religiously wrote in her journal and turned it in to Ms Harley on a weekly basis. She shared an excerpt of her journal and asked me whether or not her journal content could be construed as sounding disrespectful to Ms Harley. She read to me the following excerpt:

> [The students] in the second period need more instruction than I thought. They needed the teachers to help them with the pace and reflect on each session and make predictions. They needed to be asked questions after each session, so that they could adjust their understanding and raise individual questions that cause misunderstandings when they read. Book report is a very effective way to evaluate students' comprehension and sometimes, develop students' writing skills. However, it can be overwhelming for many ESOL II students. They need [explanation and clarification] before doing it independently. If the teachers could go over the gist of the story by using a story map to organize class discussion so that students can know what to write and how to write it. High school students are complicated in terms of cultural backgrounds, and they need more time to work by themselves. I know that it is important for them to work by themselves, but how teachers play positive role in their learning influences students' attitudes as well as academic performance at school. (Interview, 3/15)

She realized that she needed to change the last part of the above excerpt so as not to sound too harsh, as if she were suggesting a different pedagogy for Ms Harley. Although she wanted to return to Ms Tomiko's mentorship, Xia was looking forward to taking over Ms Harley's class to show her what 'teaching' was all about. '[I]n two weeks, I am going to take over the classes and probably I will show her what teaching is' (Interview, 3/15).

'It was really tough unless I spoke their native languages …'

In 2004, Yu Ri sought out two different volunteer teaching opportunities as a way to introduce herself to learning to teach. She wanted to get a taste of teaching before she began her student teaching experience in the spring of 2005. Her first volunteer teaching experience was in an adult ESL course, which met once a week in a church-based program for newly arrived immigrants and family members from African and Hispanic countries. Her second volunteer teaching experience was teaching the Korean language once a week to interested adult NESs and heritage Korean speakers. During these months of volunteer teaching, she realized the value of teaching in relation to different learning and second language acquisition theories learned in her TESOL program courses.

Yu Ri's low-level beginner class in the church-based ESL program was challenging. Yu Ri was not able to do a needs analysis of her students, since 'it [was] really tough unless I [spoke] their native language' (Interview, 1/31). Yu Ri introduced them to some daily greeting phrases, and showed them pictures of different pieces of furniture, since they were interested in learning about discourse of shopping because of their new immigrant status in the US. In addition to teaching them phrases and vocabulary words, and the pictures that accompanied them, she also played tapes and conversations in which they could hear native English-speaker pronunciations. Yu Ri said that since it was a free class, students were not that committed and some were absent more than not.

Yu Ri believed that it was important to make the language simple and to prepare the instructions before the actual lesson when dealing with novice beginner students. In addition, she thought that being able to speak another language might have been helpful: 'Sometimes using students' native language in class can be effective. I think TESOL program explain[s] that you should use English even though you are teaching low beginners. But I am curious or suspicious whether it is really effective' (Interview, 3/14). This suspicion of 'needing' to only speak English became even stronger as she experienced teaching English to the beginner students and teaching Korean to beginners. Yu Ri compared her teaching of beginner English to beginner Korean. 'I am teaching Korean to low beginners and I use English. I think it is unfair to teach Korean with English instruction because they are low beginners. Even though I want to teach them in Korean, they would not understand it' (Interview, 3/14). Thinking back to what her TESOL program courses had emphasized in terms of using English to teach English, she wanted the freedom to teach Korean using Korean. But this became rather difficult, just as it was difficult for Yu Ri to have English conversations with the church-based English class students. However, in Korean class, she had more chances to talk to them about their daily lives in English. Because little interaction occurred in a language that they both understood in the church-based ESL class, she did not feel as close to them as she did with the Korean class students.

'Because I grew up in an environment where teachers were expected to teach ... students supposed to study hard ...'

Yu Ri's student teaching practicum in a public high school during spring 2005 consisted of 30 hours of observation, teaching five lessons and being videotaped for three of the five lessons. Initially, Yu Ri felt intimidated about the prospect of teaching a class, being videotaped and having mentor teachers observe her teaching. Yu Ri believed that most adults came to learn because they were motivated, and thus, she expected these high school students, as near adults, to be 'into' school and to study hard. However, when she did not see that in classes, she attributed their lack of interest to the fact that public education was free. She also thought that perhaps their parents were not interested enough or that they were not pushing their children to work hard in school. 'Because I grew up in an environment where teachers were expected to teach and students were supposed to study hard, maybe yeah, that could be part of my expectations' (Interview, 2/23). She attributed her expectations of the students she encountered in the student teaching context to the way that she had learned in high school in Korea. Yu Ri saw some good model teaching in some classes, but in others, she did not witness any 'teaching'. In a particular class, she expected the teacher to 'teach' something.

> The class was divided into groups, where they did silent reading of each chapter followed by a student summarization of the meaning of the story. There was no teacher instruction going on in small groups. I did not observe any teaching so I was kind of disappointed. Maybe she is a good teacher, but I could not see her teaching, I don't know, so I can't tell whether she has good instruction or not. (Interview, 2/23)

Yu Ri equated 'teaching' with teacher-directed lessons rather than with group work and/or individual work. After observing for several weeks, Yu Ri questioned, 'Why do these students come to school? Why do they get up so early to come to school?' She did not see any lessons apparent in classes; teachers did not force students to learn anything; and lessons were slow-paced. Yu Ri was not quite sure whether or not the students had been learning, since she saw very few teacher-directed lessons.

On a positive note, Yu Ri was surprised to see ESL teachers teaching content at this high school, which was different from her middle school experience in New York. She thought that it was great to be able to explain the lessons or materials in a way that the ESL population would understand through content ESL. An example of a teacher-directed lesson occurred in a content ESL class, and Yu Ri noted that this teacher was actually 'teaching'. An economics class watched a video, followed by the teacher questioning students on the content. Also, she learned about disciplining disruptive students who were not paying attention in class. To Yu Ri, this was about learning, since there was a clear role for the teacher as an authority figure.

'I am not sure why they should come to school to learn so early ...'

When Yu Ri blurted out, 'I am not sure why they should come to school to learn so early in the morning [if they're not being taught anything]', she may have been conceptualizing learning based on what she had been accustomed to in the Korean educational setting, which differed markedly from what she had been observing in the US public educational system. Generally speaking, Yu Ri thought that teachers in the US did not force the students to learn. In particular, Yu Ri's conception of 'not academic' in observing the high school students' classes was that, in contrast to American university settings, no academic questions were asked. These would include questions pertaining to reading comprehension and other questions that made students think critically about the topic being discussed. There was very little academically oriented discussion in high school classrooms. She stated the following:

> They just explained something and the classroom was not structured in that there would be different ways to control what the students were learning. Not all classes had some kind of worksheets to check whether they had learned or not. They were not focused on academics, but perhaps were more interested in obtaining specific skills. (Interview, 2/23)

In Korea, Yu Ri would see the same situations of teaching and learning in vocational schools, but not in Korean public schools or colleges. The reason for this was that the purpose of vocational schools in Korea was not to go to college, but to learn specific trades or skills to get a job after graduation.

Yu Ri's overall impression of her student teaching assignment at the high school was that it served as 'a good experience to get up early in the morning. I felt that students were more open to me due to my NNES status' (Interview, 3/2). Some students talked about the fact that they felt disadvantaged because their language was not good. There were open conversations among high school students about what they were thinking. They asked her questions about college life and what she learned, and the logistics of attending college. Her assumptions about them wanting to get a job right after high school were disproved when they asked her questions related to her academic work and lifestyle as a college student. She talked to them about the college application process, her experience studying in Korea, studying in the US for the last two years of college and professors' attitudes toward international students. Furthermore, her student teaching experience helped her envision that content ESL was possible. In addition, most of the high school students she met, she thought, may not be fully supported by their parents for studies, but the school system provided a translation system and an academic support system for students who fell behind. In Korea, if students got poor grades, it was the students' fault, but in the US, teachers and administrators tried to find out the reasons behind the students' poor academic behavior to get to the root of the problem (Interview, 3/14).

Knowledge Constructed In and Out of TESOL Programs into the Student Teaching Classrooms

The women's privileged yet turbulent journeys from their home countries to the US brought forth many ways in which the women perceived and positioned themselves as NNES multilinguals and as English teachers in the US. The irony is that the English language and the women's mastery of it in their home countries brought for them a sense of belonging and a symbolic form of empowerment, as well as cultural and social capital. However, these privileged forms of their linguistic identities were shattered once they entered the US educational contexts. It is these contentions of language and teacher identity that are at the core of the three women's narrative accounts presented in this chapter. The remainder of the chapter aims to theorize each woman's English language and teacher identity.

Liu's language and race at the center of being marginalized in the US

Unfortunately for Liu, the 'full of magic!' confidence was shaken when she became matriculated into the TESOL program. Liu's construction of self as an NNES, and negotiation of herself to be a legitimate TESOL student and ultimately an educator, were constrained by the dominant discourse that upheld the erroneous notion that only white NESs would be ideal English teachers (Giampapa, 2004; Hansen, 2004). Furthermore, Liu's experience in working on a TESOL program project with one of her professors and a doctoral student constrained the ways in which she perceived her linguistic and racial identities. Liu felt that her contributions on the program project would have been taken seriously if she were a white NES graduate student. Liu's experience resonated with what Miller (2004: 311) states, in that 'speaking constructs aspects of our identities, but requires the collaboration of the listener, who must not only hear, but as Bourdieu (1991) points out, must also believe'. I must add that the believing did not occur as a result of native speakerist ideology embedded in who is seen as credible and authentic. According to Liu, the professor and the doctoral student, though *hearing her* talk about the discrepancy she saw in the data for the program project, did not believe her, and perhaps racialized her statement, as indicated by statements such as, 'No, I don't think so' (Interview, 2/28). Liu's decision was to stay silent and not to push her case any further, which is consistent with the role expected of a woman from a traditional Chinese family and also with her legitimate comment that 'silence resists' (Interview, 2/28).

Liu's comment parallels Hurtado's (1996) notion that silence could be a powerful tool for many women of color. Hurtado (1989, cited in Hurtado, 1996: 382) states, 'Many women of Color use silence with a specific goal in mind and return to their own safe communities to share what they have learned and to verify the accuracy of their observations'. Furthermore, what Liu attributed to be rejection by the professor and doctoral student because of her language abilities could have related simply to an issue of over-inflated egos, specifically, two individuals who just believed that a master's-level student could not be right with regard to finding a solution to a problem for which they themselves struggled to find the solution. However, from Liu's perspective, her linguistic identity and her racial identity were at the center of this problem. Liu saw herself stepping back from being an active participant in a program project. She saw these pull-backs as linked to perceptions of inadequate English communications skills, and she bottled up her feelings as a result of this marginalization.

Liu stated that even if academic knowledge levels were equivalent, international NNES students would still be looked down upon because of this language–birth discrepancy, namely, Liu's native language was not English, and she was not from the Inner Circle countries (Amin, 2001; Kachru, 1987). For Liu, this incident became a racialized event, in that language and race were interlaced and further subjugated her (Kubota & Lin, 2006). The discursive practices of individuals who promote nativist ideology perceive women such as Liu as NNESs, outsiders to the core of TESOL communities and learners of the English language, who can never reach the identity of an ESL teacher (Amin, 2001). Because of this class divide, she felt compelled to participate more in classroom discussions (i.e. to become more vocal at times), and tried to break into other learning communities. Hurtado (1996) discusses vocalness or outspokenness as one of the strategies for women of color. She states, 'Outspokenness is the complement of the strategy of silence. Knowing when to talk and just what to say are effective if individuals are not expected to talk. It is the surprise attack that has the most impact' (Hurtado, 1996: 382). In particular, Liu was asserting her right to establish herself as an active peripheral participant in the program, as opposed to remaining a marginalized participant, a role she had been relegated to by others within the program.

Liu's reimagining of her teacher identity

> I feel the longer I stay in the education program, the more interest I have in dealing with children. When I came into the middle school and elementary school, I have some kind of feeling in my heart that I have never found before. I think that I might change my career in the future and when I stay with them. I feel naïve as they are. I feel very relaxed and very happy. I always had dreams of being a very successful woman, and do something very successful in the field. I never thought about being a common person, a teacher. I feel that when I face these kids, they are like my children, especially the special education student I tutored. I wish I could be with him every day, so that I could help him, and he will not be down. (Interview, 4/27)

Liu shared this excerpt with me upon completing her first three weeks of her pre-student teaching experience. Because Liu had never thought about teaching children, she never imagined that she would feel moved by her pre-student teaching experience in an elementary ESL classroom. She stated that being an elementary school teacher would be one of her future options upon returning to China. In sharing this newfound vision, Liu was reminded of what her parents told her when she was in high school and thinking about college majors and a future career. They wanted her to be a teacher because it was perceived to be an easy job by her parents. Since Liu was born with some health issues, her parents always wanted her to protect herself. Liu never took her parents' suggestions seriously. 'I strongly protested their idea [of me being a teacher]. I will never do a job like that because I thought that I had some ability to do something better than that. It is common in China that if people cannot get into good schools, good universities, then they go to teachers' college or nursing school' (Interview, 4/27). Teachers' college did not require high scores, but Liu's scores for college entrance were extremely high. Her parents had certain expectations for Liu because she had health problems, and she was their only child. Liu invoked her vision of teacher identity in general, and language teacher identity in particular, to her parents as a career path that was beneath her abilities. However, after working with a mentor teacher in her student teaching capacity, Liu began to shift her perceptions and embrace her imagined language teacher identity (e.g. Clark, 2008; Kearney, 2013; Olsen, 2008; Sinner, 2013). But, more importantly, her work with elementary and middle school children began to shape her perspectives on elementary school teaching ideology that was part of her Chinese lived experiences. One could argue that this imagined teacher identity was never part of her passion because she had never interacted with teaching children in the first place until she came to embark on her student teaching journey. Her love for and commitment to working with children who are often perceived to be marginalized trumped her need to be perceived as a successful and legitimate career woman.

Xia's wrestling with issues of credibility in teacher identity

For Xia, this question of who claims credibility to teach English was an issue that she wrestled with throughout her stay in the US. There existed an assigned identity marker that made her realize the forces she would have to resist. This pertained to an erroneous, preconceived notion that people maintained regarding who should be teaching English and who should not be teaching English. Basically, the prevailing school of thought stipulated that one needed to claim an NES identity in order to teach English, such that NESs were perceived as the owners of the English language teaching world (Widdowson, 1994). This was something that she needed to problematize in order to prove the erroneousness of this assertion to herself and others, like the two Chinese immigrant NNESs (the temporary job contact person and her friend who laughed at her about her ESL student teaching) with whom she encountered difficulties during her studies.

A turning point came in one of the graduate courses in her program. Xia came to realize that she could also claim bilingual and ideal English speaker identities, in that there was no such person who could speak or use English perfectly. The revelation gleaned from this course gave her a newfound understanding that she too could claim ideal English speaker and teacher status, thus helping her to problematize the dominant discourse. Knowledge gained from this graduate course gave Xia the understanding that she needed in order not only to problematize the existing discourse, but also to understand where she placed herself in terms of this prevailing discourse. This experience of being able to problematize the existing discourse was what she had yearned for in coming to a program to learn new ways of constructing knowledge. For Xia, a new way of constructing knowledge included her lived experiences and the balancing of her complex identities in the making of herself as a legitimate and highly qualified English teacher. Her strong sense of scholarliness and burgeoning professional identity led her to seek a program dedicated to promoting learning for the sake of learning and imparting knowledge, as opposed to simply conferring a degree.

Xia's validation of her teacher identity

It was through her student teaching experience under an NNES mentor teacher that Xia was able to validate her sense of teaching identity and was able to gain self-confidence as an NNES ESL teacher. Working with Ms Tomiko, Xia was able to gain much more in the way of teaching tools. Xia noted that teaching ESL has as much to do with the attitude that one exhibits toward one's students as it does with how well one speaks English.

With this growth stemming from her educational and teaching experiences, Xia finally recognized that being a bilingual NNES and addressing the needs of her students was as important, if not more important, than being proficient in the usage of the English language.

With her confidence burgeoning under the tutelage of Ms Tomiko, Xia went through an identity transformation, where she developed a strong sense of identity as an NNES in addition to being a very able teacher. The two identities were equally important in her professional development. She commented on the fact that her identity as an NNES was equally important to her, if not more important, than her identity as an ESL teacher. While working with Ms Tomiko, she realized that Ms Tomiko also had to work hard in order to establish legitimacy and credibility for herself as a qualifying ESL teacher, unlike bilingual NES teachers from dominant racial groupings. Xia stated,

> [International people] are under language pressure and other issues, like my mentor teacher. They need to work harder to prove that they are qualified for the position. That really bothers me. If you want to work here, they have to do that because you don't have many choices here. (Interview, 1/25)

Xia's statement about NNES ESL teachers working hard was also echoed by the participants in Amin's (2004) study. The visible minority teachers in Amin's study discussed the many hours of hard work they put into overcoming their perceived weaknesses. As one teacher stated about her experience:

> [The students] soon realize that it's not just the color of the skin. Is she a good teacher? That is the bottom line. Your reputation [as a teacher] gets around. If you are a dedicated teacher and you are doing a good job, then the word gets around and then there will be no problems. (Amin, 2004: 72)

Due to this professional relationship, Xia's confidence level was boosted, and she knew that she could also do it, thus overcoming the erroneous, preconceived notion held by many in society regarding who should teach English to ELLs in the public school system. In essence, Xia's student teaching experience in Ms Tomiko's class brought her to a new level of understanding about her teacher identity as an NNES. However, her experience with the high school mentor teacher, Ms Harley, was not as helpful as with Ms Tomiko. Xia's statement about her interaction, or lack of interaction, with Ms Harley resonated with the pedagogy gained from Ms Tomiko's class, where both Ms Tomiko and Xia were active in engaging student learning: 'I know [Ms Tomiko] is exceptional. I did not expect that this second mentor teacher would be as good as she is, but at least, she should go through all the steps in giving a lesson. [I]t is not giving a lesson. Go back to your seat and do whatever you want' (Interview, 3/15).

> Book report is a very effective way to evaluate students' comprehension and sometimes, develop students' writing skills. However, it can be overwhelming for many ESOL II students. They need [explanation and clarification] before doing it independently. If the teachers could go over the gist of the story by using a story map to organize class discussion so that students can know what to write and how to write it. High school students are complicated in terms of cultural backgrounds, and they need more time to work by themselves. I know that it is important for them to work by themselves, but how teachers play positive role in their learning influences students' attitudes as well as academic performance at school. (Interview, 3/15)

The above excerpt from one of the journal entries illustrates what it was that the teacher needed to do in order to guide students in the classroom, according to Xia. It also highlights how the instruction should have been carried out in the classroom. Indirectly, Xia imposed her own pedagogy on Ms Harley, which was the pedagogy gleaned from Ms Tomiko's class, as well as from her own learning journey. Basically, her student teaching experiences in two contexts were at the heart of her truly understanding and identifying herself as a teacher and also understanding that ESL teachers come in all types. All of her life events had converged, enabling her to see herself as one who was going to make significant contributions to the field of TESOL. Xia maintained a very strong sense of what teaching should be like and what teachers should do in order to promote learning for all students, especially multilingual students.

Yu Ri's conceptions of ideal student images and language pedagogy

Without having had any contact with high school students beforehand as a teacher, Yu Ri commenced her student teaching experience. Yu Ri had a clear understanding of what her students should be like in the classroom and in relation to their work ethics, since her formulation of high school student identity came from her own experiences as a high school student in Korea. She allowed this to shape her image of their learning potentials and aspirations beyond high school. Yu Ri stated that she had assumed that these high school students would be motivated, as was the case for herself as a student and her ESL adult students, whose motivation to learn the language was for the purpose of survival as immigrants in this country. However, after spending nearly one semester with these high school students from diverse linguistic and cultural backgrounds, she learned that many of these students were in fact, enthusiastic learners, who liked the fact that she was also an NNES similar to themselves. They even asked her numerous questions about college and applying to colleges.

Another preconceived notion that Yu Ri brought to her student teaching experiences was that English should be taught using English, which differed from how she had been taught English in Korea. Yu Ri interpreted this to have been a mis-educative experience (Dewey, 1938). This notion was upheld throughout her volunteer teaching experience, in which she had to teach English to newly arrived immigrants using English for practical considerations, but also, English was the only common language which Yu Ri and her students shared. However, she noted that teaching Korean to native English students and heritage Korean speakers using English was not consistent with the teaching philosophy that dictated that the language being taught should also be the language of instruction. This was similar to her experience in learning English in Korean.

Through her coursework and her student and volunteer teaching experiences, Yu Ri came to construct new ways of understanding TESOL knowledge and pedagogy. First and foremost, the context in which English is being learned and taught is critical. Yu Ri learned English in the Korean educational system using Korean, and taught Korean in the US educational system using English, because these were considered subjects of study. However, she had to teach newly arrived immigrants in English, as this was the only vehicle available for daily communication with all of these students.

Second, students' linguistic proficiency levels dictated which language to use for pedagogy. Because the church-based students and the students in the Korean language class were beginner-level students, the common language of both the teacher and the students had to be used for language instruction. Furthermore, Yu Ri realized that being a teacher is more than enacting language pedagogy. It is also about advocacy. Prior to commencing her student teaching experiences, Yu Ri maintained the viewpoint, as per her experience as a student in the Korean public educational system, that teachers were not responsible for helping students to get to the roots of their problems. This was the responsibility of the students and their families, not the teachers. From her student teaching experiences, she noted that teachers in the US do help students to get to the roots of their problems, unlike in Korea. Yu Ri embraced this relationship that she could build with her students in her future teaching situations upon returning to Korea. Finally, Yu Ri came to realize that it is only through practicing teaching that teachers will come to understand the theory-and-practice connection.

Imagined Teacher and Professional Identities

Even with their master's degrees in TESOL and different teaching experiences, the women noted that there might be challenges in securing teaching positions once they returned to their countries. Liu noted that she might not find a job immediately, due to only having a master's degree. She observed that there were many people with master's degrees from English-speaking countries in China. She thought that it would be beneficial to find a job in Beijing. If there were no job availabilities for her in high-ranking universities, then she would look into foreign corporations. Her master's program would qualify her for positions other than in English education. Liu said that she would like to be in some business related to education; to help her husband with his international trade business; or to do some work with a previous employer, integrating specific technological skills into the Chinese market. She was looking forward to such opportunities in China. She felt that she may need to get her PhD at some point in her life, but for now, she '[did not] want to lose so many opportunities for a PhD. I need to know why I want to do a PhD' (Interview, 2/28). As for Xia, she realized that there were outside forces unbeknownst to her that surfaced in her own student teaching experiences, which might also be the case in teaching English in China. Xia was exposed to numerous mandates and standards, such as the National State Standards (NSS). She realized that practically all educational systems are bound by certain sets of standards and mandates, which limit what one can do or even expect to do with respect to educational reforms. Xia realized that teaching would require engaging in a balancing act between what was within one's control and what was not within one's control. She realized that she would need to balance what she wanted to do in the classroom environment with what she would have to do as mandated by states or other jurisdictions (Nunan, 2003). With Yu Ri, while she was thankful for the opportunities given to her to do her student teaching in a high school ESL setting that promoted content ESL (teaching of academic subjects using ESL pedagogies to ESL students), it was different from what she would encounter in Korea. Yu Ri's comments paralleled Brinton's (2004) discussion of challenges faced by TESOL programs when it came to accommodating their NNES students who planned to return to their native countries to teach English.

A critical theme that emerged from Liu, Xia and Yu Ri was focused on how their field experience transformed their language teacher identities. For all three of them, mentor teachers played an indispensable role in shaping their language teacher identities. Within a very short period of time (no more than a semester), each woman began to understand the TESOL theory-and-practice connection introduced in their graduate TESOL courses. While all three women had challenges that needed to be overcome in their own programs, when they entered their student teaching settings, their entire focus shifted to being mentored by classroom teachers, designing lessons and interacting with the students. In many ways, the student teaching contexts were a fertile ground that helped them transform their imagined teacher identities.

In the Epilogue, I bring the thematic discussions emerging from Han Nah, Liu, Xia and Shu-Ming to that of my 'unfinished' autobiographic inquiry. In particular, I direct attention to my pre- and post-tenure time line, in terms of unraveling my identities as a teacher-scholar working with teacher education students in the Ivory Tower. However, I also delineate the discussion around what it means to be a woman in the academy in general, and a mother in the academy in particular. While my unfinished autobiographic inquiry is only a sliver of what this book is about, without disclosing my (dis)empowered identities, I would not have been able to pen this book.

Note

(1) With the *TESOL Quaterly* and *Race, Ethnicity, and Education* journal editors' permission, sections of this chapter come from Park (2012, 2015).

6 Epilogue: Juxtaposing My Autobiographical Critical Incidents with Meanings gleaned from the Women's Narratives: Where Privilege Meets Marginalization

It is the day before the 45th presidential inauguration as I begin revising this final chapter. While I am not looking forward to the next four years with this new president, I am excited about the Women's March for Justice in Washington DC on January 21, 2017. This excitement, however, is masked by many complicated layers of emotion – excitement, because this will be my first march to demonstrate my stance on issues; frustration and anger, because even the thought of having someone like him as the next president infuriates me. *What could I/we have done more to prevent him from being elected?* This question lingers in my mind every single day, but at times, thinking that I will soon wake up from a horrible nightmare ... a wishful thinking. My anger is also complicated by fear and sadness that I have. In 2017, we are still fighting for our human dignity and rights – our rights to affordable health care; our rights to fall in love with whom it feels right; our rights to citizenship, residency and linguistic choices in spaces that bring us peace and comfort; our rights to access our mobility – and how all these justifiable rights are connected to who we are as women in this country, as human beings. The racial, gender, class and other social identity divides that historical figures such as Martin Luther King, Jr. and Mahatma Gandhi wrestled with and fought against as civil rights activists are still very present in this day and age, and these divides are continuously oppressing the nation and its people, now more than ever. More sadly, the media, currently, is filled with acts of hate, violence and ignorance, coming from those who seem to think that they are somehow empowered by the 45th president and what he stands for. The racist and inhumane nature of the 45th president's banning of Muslims from specific countries is horrific and ineffable, to say the least. While I cannot compare our experiences as women in the shifting terrain of teacher preparation in the field of teaching English to speakers of other languages (TESOL) to those of the active participants in the Women's March in DC, what is similar and critical to note is who we are and how we are perceived as women at a varying intersectional crossroads.

The Goals of the Chapter

This final chapter is atypical of most academic books published in the fields of TESOL and applied linguistics, for my goal is to bring together my personal narratives as a mother in academy and juxtapose them with the themes emerging from the stories of Han Nah, Liu, Xia, Yu Ri and Shu-Ming. As such, this chapter is a compilation of my personal narratives, triggered by what I gleaned from writing about the five women, who have influenced me in evocative ways. Specifically, my personal narratives are organized around critical incidents (#1–#4) that I have weathered since 2008, when I began my academic position at the current institution. These critical incidents illustrate what I experienced and felt as a woman scholar of color in academy. My goal in sharing these narratives is not to paint a victim narrative (Motha, 2006; Park, 2012) nor to blame any particular individuals, but to raise awareness and be critical of how women of color can be perceived and what we may experience in academy. Furthermore, as much as I love the work I do as a specialist in TESOL and applied linguistics, I am reminded of the need to be 'critical' even of the positive nature of my work, the colleagues with whom I interact and the students with whom I generate knowledge. These incidents that I share with you don't define my institution, but they point to the ways in which women, especially women of color, are (re)produced in our social world. The more we, both men and women, contest these inequitable acts and terrain, the closer we come to acting justly for one another in the spaces where we live and work. Ultimately, the more I see my position and my institution being a 'good fit' for me as an academician, the more I dare to question the 'politics of exuberant identification' (Butler, 2008, n.p.) of my program, my colleagues, my students and, ultimately, the institution that is a microcosm of the larger societal discourses that position us on the continuum of privilege and marginalization. As such, the concept of criticality is at the core of this final chapter. My attempt in this final chapter is to capture what it means to be critical, to raise critical consciousness around who we are, what we do and what we stand for, and ultimately, to know and reaffirm that there is power that comes with shared experiences across different but similar peoples in the academy. This is a reminder for me and for others that we are constantly wrestling with coexisting in both privileged and marginalized landscape. I now turn to the critical incidents.

Critical incident #1: Empowering or marginalizing new faculty (mothers) in academy? Access to (under)graduate teaching

In my first semester at my institution, I was scheduled to teach three sections of undergraduate research writing, all on Tuesdays and Thursdays. I was told that this would minimize the number of preparations for courses I teach. Yes, that was indeed true, since I only needed to prepare for one course, even though there was a total of 75 students in the three sections. I was also told that teaching three sections of one course on Tuesdays and Thursdays would minimize my need for extra day care issues for my newborn son. All in all, it was helpful, in that I wasn't juggling a M/W/F schedule; I didn't have three different preparations in one semester; and I didn't have to teach in the evenings, when most of the graduate courses were offered. However, what I realize now is that teaching three sections of undergraduate research writing in my first semester wasn't perceived as advancing my career as a new scholar in academy, but was an arrangement that prevented me from gaining access to both benefits and challenges of being a graduate faculty member in higher education. As I was hired into a specialized graduate program in the English department, and whether my hire was due to a high need or to prevent any possible lawsuit due to an unacceptable comment made during the interview process, I would never know, and it is not the focus of this critical incident.

Giving me a 'one prep' semester banned me from teaching one of my specialization courses as a TESOL teacher education specialist, in that I never got an opportunity to interact with graduate students in the program during my first semester, even though I was hired to work with and teach in a graduate program. I agree that there is an element of a probationary period for newly hired faculty, but I can't help but think about how my identity as a new mother in academy had a role in the thinking of those who scheduled me to teach certain courses in my first semester. Moreover, I often think about the unpopular nature of this course in my department, now that I have been at the current institution for about 10 years. Not many faculty members 'like' teaching the undergraduate research writing course, so why not give it to the rookie who isn't a specialist in research writing? She may or may not succeed in teaching those courses, but it does not matter, for she will probably privilege being a mother over teaching in our department. This may sound too harsh, but I can't negate my subjective lived experiences and my years of teaching in the department lend to such a critical reflection of these events as they unfolded for me.

On the other hand, I also gained much from teaching these sections in the first semester and in subsequent years (at least one section of this same course for the first 4 years at the institution). I focused on using this teaching opportunity to create a research project that helped me and my registered students to think about social justice issues. The sections I designed and taught were focused on understanding issues of social justice in disciplinary domains, which led students to think about different social (in)justice issues in their majors. My teaching of this course, and a research project that ensued, led to several presentations and publications in refereed journals (Park, 2015; Park & Amevuvor, 2015; Weinstein & Park, 2014). As a result, I learned about layers of social (in)justices being experienced by both students and faculty in programs and departments across my institutions. I was in a privileged position to interact with my students in unpacking social injustice issues and unconscious discriminatory practices that were at the core of different disciplinary spaces within and beyond the institution. For instance, due to the caliber and popularity of the Criminal Justice major in my institution, I had the privilege of having many criminology majors in my research writing course. They often discussed the difficulties for women working in the field of criminal justice, and the ways in which the media depicts women in prison. These were just a few samples that my students brought to my course. Not only did I learn from their disciplinary majors and how society at large depicts these disciplines, but I was able to share my own experiences as a woman of color in academy who specializes in TESOL, which continues to position racial and linguistic minorities as incompetent teachers of English.

I can confidently state that I learned from teaching three sections of the same course during my first semester and subsequent semesters. I didn't have the luxury of reflecting on these critical learning moments, nor did I have time to raise critical consciousness around why I was the only new faculty given three sections of the most difficult and unpopular course. However, those events empowered me to focus more on preparing for the course, pushed me to be more engaged with often silent but unruly undergraduate students and, finally, compelled me to bring together teaching and research to carve a niche for myself as a teacher scholar at my current institution.

Critical incident #2: Empowering or marginalizing new faculty (mothers) in academy?: Proctoring student evaluation

It was a few days before my week-long Thanksgiving break in November 2009. I was called into the chair's office for a meeting. I wondered why she would want to see me. I was anxious ... just because I was being called into the chair's office. The next thing I knew, I was in tears and defending my actions. According to the chair, one of my colleagues had accused me of looking at the student narratives of a faculty course evaluation that I was proctoring. I was in tears because I was being accused of something that I did not do. I continued to explain to the chair that I volunteered to proctor the faculty's course evaluation because I happened to be in my office during that time. My course evaluations were already completed by another faculty member the day before. I stated, 'This faculty and I did not even do an even swap, so why would I go out of my way to look at the student narratives? For what reason?' I continued to argue with the chair, and stated, 'There is also an assumption built into this accusation, in that we both needed assistance with our teaching evaluation. That we weren't good teachers. That for some reason, this faculty needed my help?' The chair obviously realized that I was beyond upset, and I wasn't going to drop this. Of course, I wanted to know which of my many colleagues accused a newly hired faculty like myself. What evidence did this person have? I also knew that the chair couldn't break the confidence of this faculty who wrongly accused me. The chair was just doing her job ... to present the information, and hear my side of the story. Well, she did more than that. I couldn't stop crying, and the chair just listened to me and allowed me the space to vent and state my side of the story. I must have stayed in her office for about half an hour, trying to comprehend this accusation, but it seemed like an eternity of time.

I couldn't drop this event. This was only my second year as tenure-track faculty, and someone was already out to crush my good name. I needed to let my colleagues in my doctoral program know what I just went through. I came back to my office. My eyes were puffy and I did not want to bump into anyone in the department. I was relieved to be in my office, and I couldn't stop crying. After composing myself, I started an email to my program colleagues. My goal was not to find out who accused me, but to let my colleagues know what I went through and how I was feeling as a result of this incident. In the lengthy email, I explained what had just transpired in the chair's office, and I shared my innocence by stating that there was no reason for me to do such a thing because neither one of us had anything to gain. We didn't do an even swap of course evaluations, and neither one of us needed any help with our pedagogies. The funny thing was that none of my women colleagues responded to the email. Only a couple of male colleagues responded to my email, consoling me. A few days later, we had an MA program meeting, and I confronted the faculty at that meeting, reiterating the accusation I had received. All of them in the program meeting had already received my lengthy email a few days ago, but I wanted to confront them face to face. At that time, this program was all women faculty, and some had been at the institution for more than 20 years. I was one of the two newly hired ones. A couple of the women faculty stated that I should just ignore the accusation, and let it go. That was when I got even more upset, and shouted at them, 'Would you let it go if your name was being smeared in the mud?' What have I ever done wrong in this program to deserve this kind of treatment?

To this date, I do not know who accused me, though I could surmise. My point of sharing this incident is not to expose the person who had accused me, but to argue that these types of incidents happen everywhere, and unless we (women faculty) disclose these incidents in higher education, there will never be any kind of closure. It is also about the lack of mentoring that many women faculty (and I am sure some men as well) receive in higher education. Everyone needs mentoring. A different scenario could have ensued. If this incident were true, then it would have been appropriate for a senior faculty to mentor someone like me in what it means to proctor course evaluations. It is also important to reiterate that the sharing of this critical incident is not to portray myself as a victimized woman faculty in higher education, but to raise critical awareness of how even the most minute incident (although mine was not minute) can become a lesson for those involved in advocacy and mentoring work. Furthermore, by disclosing this incident now, if I can indirectly help those who may have gone through, or are going through, similar marginalized experiences, I hope that my narrative can provide them with a sense of agency in confronting those who continue to marginalize us in the Ivory Tower. It is not appropriate to fold in these incidents. We need to discuss them, make them become part of the faculty discourse, so that more appropriate mentoring can occur in our lives in academia.

Critical incident #3: Empowering or marginalizing new faculty (mothers) in academy?: Being silenced and interrupted in public spaces

Dissertation defenses are highlights for both faculty and doctoral students, since it is a critical time for doctoral students defending their work and for faculty showcasing what they know and the results of their mentored work. Unlike the above two incidents, this incident has occurred frequently during my time at my institution. When it happened the first time, I was angry, and I still do get angry, but it is more amusing now than anything. The reason it is amusing is because it reminds me of the concept of 'mansplaining' that is often critiqued in social media. During dissertation defenses that I have been involved in, there were numerous times when I was talked over. For instance, a few of my male colleagues, well-intentioned I assume, would say something like, 'What Dr Park means is ...' And then they would continue, explaining what I had just stated. When this happened the first time, I was silenced and I thought to myself, 'Well, maybe my English is off today! Am I not making any sense for that faculty to reiterate what I just stated?' So, I was putting the blame on myself. And then it continued to happen frequently. In the beginning, it happened with the same colleague. He would say the same thing, 'What Dr Park means is ...' I am not sure how long it took me to jump into his interruption of my comments, but I did one day. It was at a final defense, and he did it again. But this time, I interrupted his interruption and, in my louder than normal voice, said, 'I am not done yet. Why are you repeating what I stated?' However, the funny (it's funny now, but it wasn't funny then) response came from the doctoral student defending her dissertation. She looked at him and stated, 'Yes, Dr_____! I understand.' And then she turned around to me and looked quizzical, even though my male colleague had repeated what I had just stated to the student.

This talking over me and interrupting my flow of ideas happened most frequently at dissertation defenses, but it also happened in smaller break-out meetings during faculty retreats, as well as in monthly program meetings. It is senior male colleagues or women colleagues, perceived to be in positions of power, who tend to interrupt my conversation or my comments. On one of these occasions, I yelled, 'I am not done talking!' This colleague looked at me as if I were from another planet. I think he understood, but the issue is, why do I have to make my points in such a manner?

Critical incident #4: Empowering or marginalizing new scholars (mothers) in academy?: Complicating the mentoring process

The final incident is all about what mentoring could look like in higher education. This has also happened more than once, and every time this has happened, I am called into the chair's office or we have a phone conversation. There are always students who contest their grades at the end of the semester. I am glad that students feel the need to do this and demonstrate their agency. Just as the students have the right to contest their grades, faculty have the right to justify their submitted grades. Every time there is a grade appeal by a student, my chair always takes the time to talk to me about the situation. He is fully aware of the fact that I don't change grades to please students, nor to make the appeals go away. I believe there were two grade appeals for two different courses (one in the beginning of my tenure-track years, and the second one more recently).

During each appeal situation, the chair and I had a lengthy discussion about the particular student who had made the appeal. I shared with the chair my assessment of the student in question. Not only did I share with the chair my weekly assessment of their work, but I also discussed the student's work ethic, grades on papers and other notes that I kept on how I had arrived at the final grade, etc. I understand that the reason the chair talks to the faculty about grade appeal is to let the faculty know that these appeals have occurred, and not to try to persuade us to change the grades. Every time I interact with the chair about one of my former students' grade appeals, I learn something new from him. The chair has been very good at explaining policies and procedures that I may not know about, instead of just assuming that I have mastered them. Even though I have been at my institution for almost 10 years, I have yet to master every detail of institutional policy. Yes, I refer to the institution's Collective Bargaining Agreement (CBA) handbook, but the fact of the matter is that I have not mastered the contents of the CBA handbook.

The chair has always been very consistent in helping me to come to an understanding of what it means to be faculty in a state-system school in general, and in my own institution in particular. How does this particular chair's mentoring differ from the previous chair's mentoring? They are different individuals, and the ways in which each chair handles situations are very different as well. I know this is a very subjective comment, but I am beholden to who I am and what I can handle as a result of the mentoring that I have received (and not received) from my senior faculty colleagues. Both were bound by their responsibilities, but I felt attacked by the first chair. I believe, even after many years, that she may have also felt that I was guilty initially. Why does all this matter? I don't want to just focus on the gender card in these incidents with both chairs, even though it is rather ironic that I was attacked by senior women faculty at my institution. I think much has to do with how a person (in this case the department chair) handles the problem and presents the problem to the faculty (in this case, takes the time to discuss the relevance of the problem posed).

Even as I reflect on these critical incidents, I am reminded of the layers of privilege that are at the core of who I have become. However, my narrative rendering would not be complete without delineating how my privileged identity coexists with issues of marginalized incidents that have been part of my journey.

I chronicled the ways in which my privileged identity coexist(ed) with different forms of marginalization via publications (Park, 2012, 2013a, 2013b, 2015). It is in the coexistence of my privilege and marginalization that I came to understand fully the ways I was/am perceived in the academy due to my gender, my race, my language and my motherhood. Writing my 2013a piece was emotionally liberating, but more importantly, I came to acknowledge the unfinished nature of my work, as was aptly argued by Freire (1998):

> [I]t is in our incompleteness, of which we are aware, that education as a permanent process is grounded. Women and men are capable of being educated only to the extent that they are capable of seeing themselves as unfinished. Education does not make us educable. It is our awareness of being unfinished that makes us educable. And the same awareness in which we are inserted makes us eternal seekers. (Freire, 1998: 58)

The more I reread Freire's (1998) words in his *Pedagogy of Freedom*, the more I am compelled to document the world around me in the academy. In essence, Freire's (1998) words encouraged and compelled me to document the aforementioned critical incidents – my access to (under)graduate teaching, proctoring of students' evaluations, being silenced and interrupted in public spaces, and complicating the mentoring processes could have happened to anyone in academy, and such things do happen elsewhere and everywhere in the Ivory Tower. I am clear that my narration of the events experienced, witnessed and read about in the academy is just one version of many possible interpretations; I cannot negate the evocative ways in which these events make me feel and haunt me to share our collective stories. I am an 'eternal seeker', who continues to 'sanction teaching for equity, access, and social justice' (Park, 2013a: 16) in general, and endorse my multilingual teacher identity in order to combat native-speakerism and other hegemonic labels of ideal English teacher identity (Braine, 1999; Park, 2012; Phillipson, 1992; Varghese *et al.*, 2016) in particular. I include the above excerpts (Freire, 1998; Park, 2013a) in order to remind myself publicly of the work that I must continue to do as a mama teacher-scholar in the academy. Specifically, these critical incidents shared 'highlight various power structures that are prevalent in academia' (Baxley, 2012: 54). For me, rendering of these critical incidents is evocative in nature, 'creating an emotional connection with the reader(s) and engaging in emancipatory discourse that breaks the silence for people who are Othered' (Baxley, 2012: 54).

While I can only speak for my experiences at my institution, mama teacher-scholars in the academy around the world continue to wrestle with the societal-level discourses that continue to disenfranchise us due to our differing identities of gender, race, class, language and sexual orientation. These differing identities are often manifested in a complex web of power structures that are inherent in the hierarchical nature of academia. To reiterate my point, my goal is not to name the individuals who I have wrestled with in the academy, but to raise critical consciousness around incidents that could potentially happen, or have happened, to those in academia, as one way to examine our conscience in promoting and engaging in advocacy work. Coupled with these critical incidents are the themes that emanate from the narratives of Han Nah, Liu, Xia and Yu Ri, documented in Chapters 4 and 5 of this book

The critical incidents I have shared could happen to anyone at any institution, for the incidents are part of master narratives that continue to dictate certain inequitable practices in higher education. It is a reminder that there are certain gatekeepers in higher education who continue to shut the door on those striving to be part of the academic community. My goal is to share openly what I went through as one way to come to understand how various identities are minimized and contested in higher education. Just as Han Nah, Liu, Xia, Yu Ri and Shu-Ming went through different forms of privilege and marginalization in their journeys as US TESOL program candidates, I have gone through many experiences, as evident in the critical incident narratives shared. Just because I am tenured faculty does not mean that these incidents cease. These marginalizing incidents are part of being in the Ivory Tower. It is part of being a woman in the academy. It is part of being a minority woman in the academy. And, it certainly is part of being perceived as a mother in the academy. Although I have accepted these societal-level discourses that continue to disenfranchise women in the academy, this acceptance does not mean that I will cease to raise critical consciousness by sharing them publicly. I will continue to fight those who consciously and unconsciously negate the ethnic, racial and gendered epistemologies that are part of the diverse body of higher education (Ladson-Billings, 2000).

Would I have been treated differently if I were a dominant image in the predominantly white institution of higher learning? How would other women in general, and other women of color in particular, respond to such incidents? Equally important questions are: How do they see me as a mother of a young child? How does my mothering identity identify me as a scholar in the academy? I would probably be seen as an individual making too big a deal of these incidents. But the fact of the matter is that my gender, race and language DO matter; and it is in trying to understand how issues of power, privilege and status (or lack thereof) play out in these intersectional relationships that I am compelled to share these incidents. In trying to come to grips with these narrativized incidents, it is important to understand that there is no singular Truth in what we experience in our lives. What occurs and how we feel about the experiences become part of our ontological and epistemological perspectives. It is important to understand that what I have felt and experienced at these specific moments are legitimate, and that these very experiences have become part of discourses that continue to privilege some and marginalize others. More importantly, these discourses of privilege AND marginalization are also part of my fluid and complicated identities-in-practice.

The abovementioned narrativized incidents, among others that have not been storied in this book, have been a critical component of who I am and have become as a teacher educator. Just as I could have been mentored in a different way instead of being called into the chair's office, Han Nah, Liu, Xia and Yu Ri could have been mentored differently instead of having had to go through the marginalizing experiences discussed in Chapters 4 and 5 of this book. Han Nah was left alone to find her niche in her PhD program in Turkey. The Turkish professors and her classmates in the PhD program did not see her as a legitimate PhD student, and left her to continue to hone her Turkish language skills instead of pulling her into the PhD research community. I am not quite sure why Han Nah acquiesced to focusing just on improving her Turkish language skills, other than not seeing herself as someone who would marry into the Turkish community and become a legitimate member. However, the fact of the matter is that Han Nah could have invested much more into her short PhD program journey than just focusing on language skills if she had been mentored by her Turkish professors. I am sure that Han Nah being a 'foreign' woman did not help her legitimacy as a doctoral student researcher in Turkey.

Similarly, instead of undermining Liu's response to the project she joined mid-way, her TESOL program professor and a doctoral student collaborating on the project could have asked Liu follow-up questions, and attempt to understand Liu's responses to the project queries. According to Liu, her ideas were immediately dismissed by the professor and the doctoral student. Xia's experience with the part-time testing administrator wrongfully dismissed her because she was an international graduate student. The fact that Xia's Chinese accent and her race predetermined her lack of credibility to assess the tests continued to make her feel less than qualified as a TESOL professional. Finally, Yu Ri could have had more mentored learning to teach throughout her student teaching experiences instead of being left to figure things out for herself. These incidents are just a few examples of what the women experienced throughout their US educational journeys. All of these incidents could have played out very differently if each woman had been mentored appropriately. Furthermore, the incidents that I weathered and the experiences of Han Nah, Liu, Xia and Yu Ri are all part of larger, societal-level discourses of how certain identities are praised and how others are disenfranchised. Race, language, gender and class are important constructs in understanding how individuals act in certain ways, and the narratives in this book are an example of centering these identities.

In the beginning of my tenure-track faculty days, I thought that these incidents were something that only I went through and no one else had to overcome these issues. Well, the more I read about what happens in the Ivory Tower, the more I am convinced that there are racialized, gendered, and linguistic issues that continue to privilege certain individuals over others. My intentions for sharing these critical incidents are to raise these issues. These are familiar occurrences that need to be disclosed in public venues to let individuals within and beyond the academy know that these discourses are not appropriate, so that we may all learn from each other in mentoring each other and those who enter our classrooms.

Appendix A

Guidelines for Electronic Reflective Autobiographical Narratives

The goal of this electronic autobiographical narrative section is to allow you to construct a short personal history that describes what led you to a US master's in teaching English to speakers of other languages (TESOL) teacher preparation program. The following questions will offer you a better understanding of what to address in your autobiographical narrative.

Directions: Please use the following questions that pertain to your history prior to gaining admission to a master's in TESOL program to craft your narrative. Use the body of the email text or the attachment. Although there is no page limit to this narrative, it would be important to try to address all the questions below. Please respond directly under each prompt. If I need further clarification, I will email you with specific questions. I want to thank you in advance for sharing your thoughts.

Writing Prompts[1]:

Part I

Section I: Value of the English language education in your native country

(1) How is teaching English as a foreign language (TEFL) or teaching English as a second language (TESL) viewed in your country?
(2) Who has access to the English language learning in your country?
(3) Who has access to the English language teaching in your country?
(4) How are women EFL teachers (native English speakers) viewed in your native country?
(5) How are women EFL teachers (nonnative English speakers) viewed in your native country?
(6) I am assuming that most EFL teachers in your native country are nonnative English speakers. How does this affect the way the English language teaching profession is viewed in your native country?
(7) How does the above affect you as an East Asian (e.g. Chinese, Japanese, Korean, Taiwanese) woman in your country?

Section II: Your English language learning journey in your native country

(8) When did you first become interested in learning English in your native country?
(9) What personal attributes of yours made you feel specially suited to learning English in your native country?
(10) What features of learning English most appealed to you? Which features least appealed to you?
(11) What was your experience learning English like?
(12) Where did you learn the language?
(13) Who did you learn it from? Describe your English teacher and other classmates.

Section III: Your English language teaching journey in your native country
(Only answer the following questions if you have taught English)

(14) When did you first become interested in teaching English in your native country? What factors most contributed to your decision?
(15) What personal attributes of yours made you feel specially suited to teach English in your native country?
(16) What features of teaching English most appealed to you? Which features least appealed to you?
(17) What was your teaching English experience like? Where did you teach? Who were your students? Describe your teaching colleagues and textbooks/curriculum used for your classes.

Part II

Section I: Your English language learning journey in the US
(Only answer the questions that apply to you)

(18) Describe your English language learning experiences in the US. What were your teachers and your classmates like?
(19) How did it feel compared to learning English in your native country?
(20) How do you think others viewed you?

Section II: Your English language teaching journey in the US
(Only answer the questions that apply to you)

(21) How did you become interested in teaching English in the US? What factors most contributed to your decision to teach in the US?
(22) Describe your English language teaching experience in the US. Where did you teach? Who did you teach? How did other teachers and students view you, do you think?
(23) How did it feel compared to teaching English in your native country?

Section III: Your admission into the US TESOL program

(24) Why are you in a TESOL program?
(25) What are some of your significant English language learning and teaching experiences that have led you to a TESOL program path?
(26) Why did you decide to pursue a degree program at your current institution, as opposed to other institutions in the US or in other countries?
(27) What does pursuing a master's degree in the US mean to you as an East Asian woman who speaks your native tongue?
(28) What is your ultimate goal for pursuing a master's in US TESOL?
(29) What are your academic and professional needs? In other words, what do you see yourself doing after you finish the program?
(30) Where does what you know about TESOL or English language teaching (ELT) come from before coming to your current program?
(31) How would your master's in TESOL degree be valued in your native country?

Section IV: Demographics

(32) When were you born?
(33) Where were you born?
(34) What grades (formal education) did you complete in your native country?
(35) What is your marital status?
(36) Do you live with any members of your family or relatives in the US?
(37) How long have you been in the US as a student?
(38) Is your status 'international student'?
(39) How long have you been a student in the current TESOL program?
(40) About how many (what percentage approximately) of your classmates or students in the program are nonnative English speakers? What countries are they originally from?
(41) About how many (what percentage approximately) of your classmates or students in the program are females?
(42) How did you describe your TESOL program when you first entered the program?
(43) How would you describe your TESOL program now?

Note

(1) These questions have been adapted from the first assignment in one of my graduate seminar classes, 'Theory and Research on Teaching', taken in fall 2001.

Appendix B

Guidelines for Electronically Journaling Educational Incidents

The goal of this exercise is to have you journal your educational incidents via email. This electronic journal will convey your experience while enrolled in a master's in teaching English to speakers of other languages (TESOL) program.

Definition of Educational Incidents

Educational incidents are situations that occur in your academic, personal and professional contexts that may be thought-provoking and/or may trigger a memory of other incidents that have happened in your past educational experience. Your journal of reflections will help reveal your thoughts and experiences as you live (or have lived) through your program.

Directions

These educational incidents will be made up of phrases, sentences and brief paragraphs that describe situations and experiences.

that have occurred

(a) in your graduate TESOL classes;
(b) during interactions with faculty, advisor, classmates and other administrative personnel in TESOL and non-TESOL areas;
(c) while completing class assignments, projects and other programmatic structure outlined in your program;

around

(a) your understanding of the constructs of (non)native English speakers (NNES/NES);
(b) your experience as an East Asian woman;
(c) how your program will meet or not meet your future goals.

Please use the table as a guide to reflect on your experiences as you organize your thoughts of educational incidents and send them electronically on a weekly (bi-monthly) basis.

The Week of	
Where did the incident occur?	
Who was involved?	
What happened?	
Any other thoughts that were triggered by what happened	

An example of an educational incident that happened to me:

Where did the incident occur?	In a TESOL graduate seminar course in spring 2003.
Who was involved?	My interaction with one of the NNES PhD students in my program.
What happened?	In the class, we were discussing some identity issues, and I was sharing with the class my identity as an NNES professional. As soon as I made that comment, a student asked me, 'Do you identify yourself as an NNES?' My response was very short: 'Yes'. However, her question made me think about how other students in my program perceive my identity. She was reluctant to believe my claim of NNES identity. Later, she and I got together to talk more about her question to me in class. This incident led to our collaborative research project, and we have become friends and confidants in our program. After reading my autobiography, she understands why I identify myself as an NNES.
Any other thoughts that were triggered by what happened	I became more aware of how other NNES colleagues perceive me, to the point of having open conversation with other NNES friends. I also became more interested in and aware of the fact that our identities are co-constructed, meaning that we construct our identities with the text and with the sociocultural contexts we live in, but we also co-construct our identities with other people (how others perceive us). I came to understand NNESs with international student status better, in that they perhaps have more challenges and concerns than I can ever imagine. I have always been interested in this area, but this comment in my class has sparked my interest in going deeper into the world of East Asian women in TESOL programs, which has led to my dissertation study.

Appendix C

Interview Questions

The goal of this exercise is for interview questions to be used to expand what participants have narrated in their autobiographies and their journal entries. There are a set of questions, but most of the interview questions will be from a list of questions that emerged from the contents of the autobiographical narratives and the journal of educational incidents. It is my hope that the interview questions will unpack what has already been articulated in their autobiographies and journal entries in order to address the issues around pedagogy, curriculum and linguistic knowledge production in their master's in teaching English to speakers of other languages (TESOL) programs.

Interview Protocol

(a) I will ask you several demographic questions followed by questions pertaining to your understanding of native English speaking (NES) and nonnative English Speaking (NNES) constructs.
(b) I will ask you a list of questions that emerged from the content of the autobiographical narratives and journal of educational experience.
(c) Please feel free to let me know when you do not want to be audiotaped, as all interviews will be audiotaped and transcribed for the purpose of analyzing the data.

Potential Interview Questions

NES and NNES constructs:

(1) How do you see yourself in your program?
(2) How do you think others see you in your program?
(3) What kinds of images are connected to how you see yourself and how others see you?
(4) What is the meaning of 'native-ness' or 'white-ness' (being white) in TESOL?

(5) What is the meaning of 'non-native-ness' or 'Asian-ness' (being Asian) in TESOL?
(6) What does NES mean to you?
(7) What is it like being around NNESs in your program? How do they relate to you?
(8) What is it like being around NESs in your program? How do they relate to you?

Talk about any advantages or disadvantages of being in your TESOL program.

References

Adams, M., Blumenfeld, W., Casteneda, C., Hackman, H., Peters, M. and Zuniga, X. (2010) *Readings for Diversity and Social Justice*. New York: Routledge.

Amin, N. (1997) Race and the identity of the nonnative ESL teacher. *TESOL Quarterly* 31 (3), 580–583.

Amin, N. (2001) Nativism, the native speaker construct, and minority immigrant women teachers of ESL. *The CATESOL Journal* 13 (1), 89–108.

Amin, N. (2004) Nativism, the native speaker construct, and minority immigrant women teachers of English as a second language. In L. Kamhi-Stein (ed.) *Learning and Teaching from Experience: Perspectives on Nonnative English-Speaking Professionals* (pp. 61–80). Ann Arbor, MI: Michigan University Press.

Anders, S.M. (2004) Why the academic pipeline leaks: Fewer men than women perceive barriers to becoming professors. *Sex Roles* 51 (9/10), 511–521.

Aneja, G. (Fall 2016) (Non)native speakered. *TESOL Quarterly* Special Issue.

Ayers, W. (2004) *Teaching the Personal and the Political: Essays on Hope and Justice*. New York: Teachers College Press.

Barkhuizen, G. (2016) A short story approach to analyzing teacher (imagined) identities over time. *TESOL Quarterly* 50 (3), 655–683.

Bartolomé, L.I. (2009) Beyond the methods fetish: Toward a humanizing pedagogy. In A. Darder, M.P. Baltodano and R.D. Torres (eds) *The Critical Pedagogy Reader* (2nd edn). New York: Routledge.

Baxley, T.P. (2012). Navigating as an African American female scholar: Catalysts and barriers in predominantly White academia. *The International Journal of Critical Pedagogy* 4 (1), 47–64.

Belenky, M., Clinchy, B., Goldberger, N. and Tarule, J. (1997) *Women's Ways of Knowing: The development of Self, Voice, and Mind* (10th anniversary edn). New York: Basic Books.

Bell, J. (2002) Narrative research in TESOL: Narrative inquiry: More than just telling stories. *TESOL Quarterly* 36 (2), 207–213.

Berns, M. (2005) Expanding on the expanding circle: Where do WE go from here? *World Englishes* 24, 85–93. doi:10.1111/j.0883-2919.2005.00389.x

Bhattacharya, U. (2011) The 'West' in literacy studies. *Berkeley Review of Education* 2 (2), 179–198.

Bolton, K. (2005) Where WE stands: Approaches, issues, and debate in world Englishes. *World Englishes* 24, 69–83. doi:10.1111/j.0883-2919.2005.00388.x.

Bourdieu, P. (1977) *Outline of a Theory of Practice* (Vol. 16). Cambridge: Cambridge University Press.

Bourdieu, P. (1986) The forms of capital. In J. G. Richardson (ed.) *Handbook of Theory and Research for the Sociology of Education* (pp. 241–258). New York: Greenwood Press.

Bourdieu, P. (1991) *Language and Symbolic Power*. Cambridge, MA: Harvard University Press.

Bourdieu, P. and Passeron, J. (1977) *Reproduction in Education, Society, and Culture*. London: Sage Publications.

Brady, B. and Gulikers, G. (2004) Enhancing the MA in TESOL practicum course for nonnative English-speaking student teachers. In L. Kamhi-Stein (ed.) *Learning and Teaching from Experience: Perspectives on Nonnative English-Speaking Professionals* (pp. 206–229). Ann Arbor, MI: University of Michigan Press.

Braine, G. (1999) *Non-Native Educators in English Language Teaching*. Mahwah, NJ: Lawrence Erlbaum.

Braine, G. (2005) *Teaching English to the World: History, Curriculum, and Practice*. Mahwah, NJ: Lawrence Erlbaum.

Burnaby, B. and Sun, Y. (1989) Chinese teachers' views of western language teaching: Contexts informs paradigms. *TESOL Quarterly* 23 (2), 219–238.

Butler, J. (2008) Uncritical exuberance? Online article. http://www.indybay.org/newsitems/2008/11/05/18549195.php (published, November 5, 2008, no page number).

Butler, Y. (2004) What level of English proficiency do elementary school teachers need to attain to teach EFL? Case studies from Korea, Taiwan, and Japan. *TESOL Quarterly* 38 (2), 245–278.

Butler, Y. (2007) How are nonnative-English-speaking teachers perceived by young learners? *TESOL Quarterly* 33, 413–431. doi:10.2307/3587672.

Canagarajah, A.S. (2002) Reconstructing local knowledge. *Journal of Language, Identity, and Education* 1 (4), 243–259.

Carroll, S., Motha, S., and Price, J. (2008) Accessing imagined communities and reinscribing regimes of truth. *Critical Inquiry in Language Studies* 5 (3), 165–191.

Castaneda, M. and Isgro, K. (eds) (2013) *Mothers in Academia*. New York: Columbia University Press.

Clandinin, D.J. and Connelly, F.M. (2000) *Narrative Inquiry: Experience and Story in Qualitative Research*. San Francisco: Jossey-Bass, Inc.

Clandinin, D.J., Pushor, D. and Orr, A. (2007) Navigating sites for narrative inquiry. *Journal of Teacher Education* 58 (1), 21–35.

Clark, C. and Medina, C. (2000) How reading and writing literacy narratives affect preservice teachers' understanding of literacy, pedagogy, and multiculturalism. *Journal of Teacher Education* 51 (1), 63–76.

Clarke, M. (2008) *Language Teacher Identities: Co-Constructing Discourse and Community*. Clevedon: Multilingual Matters.

Cook, V. (1999). Going beyond the native speaker in language teaching. *TESOL Quarterly* 33 (2), 185–210.

Davis, K. and Skilton-Sylvester, E. (2004) Looking back, taking stock, moving forward: Investigating gender in TESOL. *TESOL Quarterly* 38 (3), 381–404.

Denzin, N. (1989) *Interpretative Interactionism*. Newbury Park, CA: Sage Publications.

Denzin, N. (2001) The reflexive interview and a performative social science. *Qualitative Inquiry*, 1 (1), 23–46.

Denzin, N. and Lincoln, Y. (2000) *Handbook of Qualitative Research* (2nd edn). Thousand Oaks, CA: Sage Publications.

Dewey, J. (1938). *Experience and Education*. New York: MacMillan.

Elbaz-Liwisch, F. (2001) Personal story as passport: Storytelling in border pedagogy. *Teaching Education* 12 (1), 81–101.

Elbaz-Luwisch, F. (2002) Writing as inquiry: Storying the teaching self in writing workshops. *Curriculum Inquiry* 32 (3), 403–428.

Evans, E. and Grant, C. (2008) *Mama, Ph.D: Women Write about Motherhood and Academic Life*. New Brunswick, NJ: Rutgers University Press.

Faez, F. (2011) Are you a native speaker of English? Moving beyond a simplistic dichotomy. *Critical Inquiry in Language Studies* 8 (4), 378–399.

Flowerdew, J. (1999) The practicum in L2 teacher education: A Hong Kong case study. *TESOL Quarterly* 33 (1), 141–145.

Flowerdew, J. (2000) Discourse community, legitimate peripheral participation, and the nonnative-English speaking scholars. *TESOL Quarterly* 34 (1), 127–150.

Flowerdew, J. and Miller, L. (2008) Social structure and individual agency in second language learning: Evidence from three life histories. *Critical Inquiry in Language Studies* 5 (4), 201–224.
Frank, A.W. (2012) Practicing dialogic narrative analysis. In J. Holstein and J. Gubrium (eds) *Varieties of Narrative Analysis* (pp. 33–52). London: Sage.
Frankenberg, R. (2001) *The Social Construction of Whiteness: White Women, Race Matters.* Minneapolis, MN: University of Minnesota Press.
Freire, P. (1998) *Pedagogy of Freedom: Ethics, Democracy, and Civic Courage.* New York: Rowman & Littlefield Publishers, Inc.
Freire, P. (2006) *Pedagogy of the Oppressed* (30th anniversary edn) (trans. Myra Bergman Ramos). New York: Continuum.
Gay, G. (2010) *Culturally Responsive Teaching: Theory, Research, and Practice.* New York: Teachers College Press.
Gao, F. (2014) Social-class identity and English learning: Studies of Chinese learners. *Journal of Language, Identity and Education* 13, 92–98.
Gee, J. (1991) Socio-cultural approaches to literacy (literacies). *Annual Review of Applied Linguistics* 12, 31–48.
Gee, J. (2004) Learning language as a matter of learning social language within discourses. In M. Hawkins (ed.) *Language Learning and Teacher Education: A Sociocultural Approach* (pp. 13–32). Clevedon: Multilingual Matters.
Giampapa, F. (2004) The politics of identity, representation, and the discourses of Selfidentification: Negotiating the periphery and the center. In A. Pavlenko and A. Blackledge (eds) *Negotiation of Identities in Multilingual Contexts* (pp. 192–219). Clevedon: Multilingual Matters.
Gordon, C. and Keyfitz, B. (2004) Women in academia: Are we asking the right questions? *Notions of the American Mathematical Society* 51 (7), 784–786.
Goto-Butler, Y.G. (2004) What level of English proficiency do elementary school teachers need to attain to teach EFL? Case studies from Korea, Taiwan, and Japan. *TESOL Quarterly* 245–278.
Goto-Butler, Y.G. (2007) How are nonnative-English-speaking teachers perceived by young learners? *TESOL Quarterly* 731–755.
Grant, R. and Wong, S. (2008) Critical race perspectives, Bourdieu, and language education. In J. Albright and A. Luke (eds) *Pierre Bourdieu and Literacy Education* (pp. 162–184). New York: Routledge.
Grimshaw, T. and Sears, C. (2008) Where am I from? Where do I belong? The negotiation and maintenance of identity by international school students. *Journal of Research in International Education* 7 (3), 259–278.
Ha, P.L. (2008) *Teaching English as an International Language: Identity, Resistance, and Negotiation.* Clevedon: Multilingual Matters.
Hale, A., Snow-Gerono and Morales F. (2008) Transformative education for culturally diverse learners through narrative and ethnography. *Teaching and Teacher Education* 24, 1413–1425.
Hanauer, D.I. (2003) Multicultural moments in poetry: The importance of the unique. *Canadian Modern Language Review* 60 (1), 69–87.
Hanauer, D. (2010) *Poetry as Research: Exploring Second Language Poetry Writing.* Philadelphia, PA: John Benjamins Publishing Company.
Hanauer, D. (2011) Meaningful literacy: Writing poetry in the language classroom. *Language Teaching* 1–11.
Hanauer, D. (2012) Meaningful literacy: Writing poetry in the language classroom. *Language Teaching* 45 (1), 105–115. doi:http://dx.doi.org/10.1017/S0261444810000522.
Hansen, J. (2004) Invisible minorities and the nonnative English-speaking professionals. In L. Kamhi-Stein (ed.) *Learning and Teaching from Experience: Perspectives on Nonnative*

English-Speaking Professionals (pp. 40–56). Ann Arbor, MI: University of Michigan Press.

Harding, S. (1987) Introduction: Is there a feminist method? In S. Harding (ed.) *Feminism and Methodology* (pp. 1–14). Bloomington, IN: Indiana University Press.

Harding, S. (1996) Gendered ways of knowing and the epistemological crisis of the West. In N. Goldberger, J. Tarule, B. Clinchy and M. Belenky (eds) *Knowledge, Difference, and Power* (pp. 431–454). New York: Basic Books.

Haroian-Guerin, G. (1999) *The Personal Narrative: Writing Ourselves as Teachers and Scholars*. Portland, ME: Calendars Island Publishers.

Hawkins, M. (2004) Social apprenticeships through mediated learning in language teacher education. In M. Hawkins (ed.) *Language Learning and Teacher Education: A Sociocultural Approach* (pp. 89–110). Buffalo, NY: Multilingual Matters.

Hendry, P. (2010) Narrative as inquiry. *The Journal of Educational Research* 103, 72–80.

Hesse-Biber, S. and Leavy, P. (2007) *Feminist Research Practice: A Primer*. Thousand Oaks, CA: Sage Publications.

Higgins, C. (2010) Gender identities in language education. In N.H. Hornberger and S. McKay (eds) *Sociolinguistics and Language Education* (pp. 370–397). Bristol: Multilingual Matters.

hooks, b. (2010) *Teaching Critical Thinking: Practical Wisdom*. New York: Routledge.

Hurlbert, C. (2012) *National Healing: Race, State, and the Teaching of Composition*. Boulder, CO: University of Colorado.

Hurtado, A. (1996) Strategic suspensions: Feminists of color theorize the production of knowledge. In N. Goldberger, J. Tarule, B. Clinchy and M. Belenky (eds) *Knowledge, Difference, and Power* (pp. 372–392). New York: Basic Books.

Ibrahim, A. (2008) Operating under erasure: Race/language/identity. *Canadian and International Education* 37 (2), 56–76.

Ivanic, R. (1998) *Writing and Identity: The Discoursal Construction of Identity in Academic Writing*. Philadelphia, PA: John Benjamins Publishing Company.

James, J.H. (2007). Autobiographical inquiry, teacher education, and (the possibility of) social justice. *Journal of Curriculum and Pedagogy* 4 (2), 161–175.

Jenkins, J. (2009) *Second Language Teacher Education: A Sociocultural Perspective*. New York: Routledge.

Jewell, M. (2003) Electronic discussion forums and English learners. *The CATESOL Journal* 15 (1), 57–64.

Jin, L. and Cortazzi, M. (1998) The culture the learner brings: A bridge or a barrier? In M. Byram and M. Fleming (eds) *Language Learning in Intercultural Perspective: Approaches through Drama and Ethnography* (pp. 98–118). New York: Cambridge University Press.

Johnson, K. and Golombek, P. (eds) (2002) *Teachers' Narrative Inquiry as Professional Development*. Cambridge: Cambridge University Press.

Johnson-Bailey, J. (2015) Race matters: The unspoken variable in the teaching-learning transaction. *New Directions for Adult and Continuing Education* 2002 (93), 39–50.

Kachru, B.B. (1987) The spread of English and sacred linguistic cows. In P.H. Lowenburg (ed.) *Language Spread and Language Policy: Issues, Implications, and Case Studies* (pp. 207–228). Washington DC: Georgetown University Press.

Kachru, B.B. (1997) World Englishes and English using communities. *Annual Review of Applied Linguistics* 17, 66–87.

Kamhi-Stein, L. (2000) Adapting US based TESOL education to meet the needs of nonnative English speakers. *TESOL Journal* 9 (3), 10–14.

Kamhi-Stein, L. (2004) *Learning and Teaching from Experience: Perspectives on Non-Native English-Speaking Professionals*. Ann Arbor, MI: University of Michigan Press.

Kamhi-Stein, L., Aagard, A., Ching, A., Paik, M.A., and Sasser, L. (2004) Teaching in kindergarten through grade 12 programs: Perceptions of native and nonnative English speaking practitioners. In L. Kamhi-Stein (ed.) *Learning and Teaching from*

Experience: Perspectives on Nonnative English Speaking Professionals (pp. 81–99). Ann Arbor, MI: University of Michigan.

Kanno, Y. (2003) *Negotiating Bilingual and Bicultural Identities: Japanese Returnees betwixt Two Worlds*. Mahwah, NJ: Lawrence Erlbaum.

Kanno, Y. (2014) Forum commentary. *Journal of Language, Identity and Education* 13, 118–121.

Kearney, E. (2013) *On Becoming a Teacher*. Boston, MA: Sense Publishers.

Kinginger, C. (2004) Alice doesn't live here anymore: Foreign language learning and identity reconstruction. In A. Pavlenko and A. Blackledge (eds) *Negotiation of Identities in Multilingual Contexts* (pp. 219–242). Clevedon: Multilingual Matters.

Kouritzin, S. (2000) A mother's tongue. *TESOL Quarterly* 34 (2), 311–324.

Kubota, R. (2004) Critical multiculturalism and second language education. In B. Norton and K. Toohey (eds) *Critical Pedagogies and Language Learning* (pp. 30–52). Cambridge: The Cambridge University Applied Linguistic Series.

Kubota, R. (2011) Questioning linguistic instrumentalism: English, neoliberalism, and language tests in Japan. *Linguistics and Education* 22, 248–260.

Kubota, R. and Lin, A. (2006) Race and TESOL: Introduction to concepts and theories. *TESOL Quarterly* 471–493.

Kubota, R. and McKay, S. (2009) Globalization and language learning in rural Japan: The role of English in the local linguistic ecology. *TESOL Quarterly* 593–619.

Kumaravadivelu, B. (1994) The postmethod condition: (E)merging strategies for second/foreign language teaching. *TESOL Quarterly* 28 (1), 27–48.

Kumaravadivelu, B. (2001) Toward a postmethod pedagogy. *TESOL Quarterly* 35, 537–560. doi:10.2307/3588427.

Kumaravadivelu, B. (2003) Problematizing cultural stereotypes in TESOL. *TESOL Quarterly* 37 (4), 709–718.

Kumaravadivelu, B. (2006) TESOL methods: Changing tracks, challenging trends. *TESOL Quarterly* 40 (1), 59–82.

Kumashiro, K.K. (2000) Toward a theory of anti-oppressive education. *Review of Educational Research* 70 (1), 25–53.

Kumashiro, K.K. (2002) Against repetition addressing resistance to anti-oppressive change in the practice of learning, teaching, supervising, and researching. *Harvard Educational Review* 72 (1), 67–91.

Ladson-Billings, G. (2000) Racialized discourses and ethnic epistemologies. In N. Denzin and Y. Lincoln (eds) *Handbook of Qualitative Research* (2nd edn) (pp. 257–278). Thousand Oaks, CA: Sage Publications.

Langman, J. (2004) (Re)constructing gender in a new voice: An introduction. *Journal Language, Identity, and Education* 3 (4), 235–244.

Lather, P. (1991) *Getting Smart: Feminist Research and Pedagogy with/in the Postmodern*. London: Routledge.

Lave, J. and Wenger, E. (1991) *Situated Learning: Legitimate Peripheral Participation*. Cambridge: Cambridge University Press.

Lee, S.J. (2005) *Up Against Whiteness: Race, School and Immigrant Youth*. New York: Teachers College Press.

Lee, S.J. (2006) Additional complexities: Social class, ethnicity, generation, and gender in Asian Americana student experiences. *Race, Ethnicity, and Education* 9 (1): 17–28.

Lee, S.J. (2009) *Unraveling the 'Model Minority' Stereotype: Listening to Asian American Youth*. New York: Teachers College Press.

Lee, S.J. and Kumashiro, K.K. (2005) *A Report on the Status of Asian Americans and Pacific Islanders in Education: Beyond the 'Model Minority' Stereotype*. Washington, DC: National Education Association, Human and Civil Rights.

Lee, E. and Simon-Maeda, A. (2006) Racialized research identities in ESL/EFL research. *TESOL Quarterly* 40 (3), 573–594.

Lee, J.K. and Park, H.G. (2001) Martial conflicts and women's identities in the contemporary Korean family. *Asian Journal of Women's Studies* 7 (4), 7–28.

Li, D. (1998) 'It's always more difficult than you plan and imagine': Teachers' perceived difficulties in introducing the Communicative Approach in South Korea. *TESOL Quarterly* 32 (4), 677–703.

Li, G. and Beckett, G.H. (2006) *"Strangers" of the academy: Asian Women Scholars in Higher Education*. Sterling, VA: Stylus Publishing.

Lillis, T. and Curry, M.J. (2010) *Academic Writing in a Global Context: The Politics and Practices of Publishing in English*. New York: Routledge.

Lin, A. (1999) Doing-English-lessons in the reproduction or transformation of social worlds? *TESOL Quarterly* 33 (3), 393–412.

Lin, A. (2004) Introducing a critical pedagogical curriculum: A feminist reflexive account. In B. Norton and K. Toohey (eds) *Critical Pedagogies and Language Learning* (pp. 271–290). Cambridge: The Cambridge University Applied Linguistic Series.

Lin, A., Wang, W., Akamatsu, N. and Medhi Riasi, A. (2002) Appropriating English, expanding identities, and revisioning the field: From TESOL to teaching English for glocalized communication (TEGCOM). *Journal of Language, Identity, and Education* 1 (4), 295–316.

Lin, A., Grant, R., Kubota, R., Motha, S., Sachs, G., Vandrick, S. and Wong, S. (2004) Women faculty of color in TESOL: Theorizing our lived experiences. *TESOL Quarterly* 38 (3), 487–503.

Lincoln, Y. and González y González, E. (2008) The search for emerging decolonizing methodologies in qualitative research: Further strategies for liberatory and democratic inquiry. *Qualitative Inquiry* 14 (5), 784–805.

Liu, D., Ahn, G., Baek, K. and Hahn, N. (2004) South Korean high school English teachers' code switching: Questions and challenges in the drive for maximal use. *TESOL Quarterly* 38 (4), 605–638.

MacDonald, S.P. (2007) The erasure of language. *College Composition and Communication* 58 (4), 585–625.

Magnet, S. (2006) Protesting privilege: An autoethnographic look at whiteness. *Qualitative Inquiry* 12, 736–749.

Margolis, J. (2008) What will keep today's teachers teaching?: Looking for a hook as a new career cycle emerges. *Teachers College Record* 110 (1), 160–194.

Mawhinney, L., Rinke, C., and Park, G. (2012) Being and becoming a teacher: How African American and White preservice teachers envision their future roles as teacher advocates. *The New Educator* 8 (4), 321–344.

McArthur, T. (2001) World English and World Englishes: Trends, tensions, varieties, and standards. *Language Teaching* 34, 1–20. doi:10.1017/S021444800016002.

McCann, C. and Kim, S. (2003) *Feminist Theory Reader: Local and Global Perspectives*. London: Routledge.

Menard-Warwick, J. (2004) I always had the desire to progress a little: Gendered narratives of immigrant language learners. *Journal of Language, Identity, and Education* 3 (4) 295–312.

Menard-Warwick, J. (2005) Intergenerational trajectories and sociopolitical context: Latina immigrants in adult ESL. *TESOL Quarterly* 39 (2), 165–186.

Menard-Warwick, J. (2009) *Gendered Identities and Immigrant Language Learning* (Vol. 4). Bristol: Multilingual Matters.

Messekher, H. (2012) Voices of pedagogy, positionality, and power: A narrative inquiry of identity and ideology (re)construction of Algerian graduate students in American universities. Unpublished doctoral dissertation, Indiana University of Pennsylvania.

Miller, J. (2004) Identity and language use: The politics of speaking ESL in schools. In A. Pavlenko and A. Blackledge (eds) *Negotiation of Identities in Multilingual Contexts* (pp. 290–315). Clevedon: Multilingual Matters.

Mills, J. (2004) Mothers and mother tongue: Perspectives on self-construction by mothers of Pakistani heritage. In A. Pavlenko and A. Blackledge (eds) *Negotiation of Identities in Multilingual Contexts* (pp. 161–191). Clevedon: Multilingual Matters.

Minichiello, V. and Kottler, J. (2010) *Qualitative Journeys: Student and Mentor Experiences with Research*. Thousand Oaks, CA: Sage publications.

Morita, N. (2004) Negotiating participation and identity in second language academic communities. *TESOL Quarterly* 38 (4), 573–604.

Motha, S.E.S. (2004) The light cast by someone else's lamp: Becoming ESOL teachers. Unpublished doctoral dissertation, University of Maryland.

Motha, S. (2006) Racializing ESOL teaching identities in US K–12 public schools. *TESOL Quarterly* 40 (3): 495–518.

Motha, S. (2014) *Race, Empire, and English Language Teaching: Creating Responsible and Ethical Anti-Racist Practice*. New York: Teachers College.

Nieto, S. (2004) *What Keeps Teachers Going?* New York: Teachers College Press.

Nieto, S. (2010) *Language, Culture, and Teaching: Critical Perspectives for a New Century*. Mahwah, NJ: Lawrence Erlbaum Associates.

Ngo, B. and Lee, S.J. (2007) Complicating the image of model minority success: A review of Southeast Asian American education. *Review of Educational Research* 7 (4), 415–453.

Noddings, N. (1987) Do we really want to produce good people?. *Journal of Moral Education* 16 (3), 177–188.

Noddings, N. (1988) An ethic of caring and its implications for instructional arrangements. *American Journal of Education* 215–230.

Norton, B. (2000) *Identity and Language Learning: Gender, Ethnicity and Educational Change*. New York: Longman.

Norton, B. (2001) Non-participation, imagined communities and the language classroom. In M. Breen (ed.) *Learner Contributions to Language Learning: New Directions in Research* (pp. 159–171). New York: Longman and Pearson Education.

Norton, B. and Pavlenko, A. (2004) Gender and English language learners: Challenges and possibilities. In B. Norton and A. Pavlenko (eds) *Gender and English Language Learners* (pp. 1–14). Alexandria, VA: TESOL.

Norton, B. and Toohey, K. (2004) *Critical Pedagogies and Language Learning*. Cambridge: Cambridge University Press.

Nunan, D. (2003) The impact of English as a global language on educational policies and practices in the Asia-Pacific region. *TESOL Quarterly* 37 (4), 589–614.

Nuske, K. (2015) Transformation and stasis: Two case studies of critical teacher education in TESOL. *Critical Inquiry in Language Studies* 12 (4), 283–312.

O'Brien, L. and Schillaci, M. (2002) Why do I want to teach, anyway? Utilizing autobiography in teacher education. *Teaching Education* 13 (1), 25–40.

O'Laughlin, E.M. and Bischoff, L.G. (2005) Balancing parenthood and academia: Work/family stress as influenced by gender and tenure status. *Journal of Family Issues* 26, 79–106.

Oda, M. (1999) English only or English plus? The language(s) of EFL organizations. In G. Braine (ed.) *Non-Native Educators in English Language Teaching* (pp. 105–121). Mahwah, NJ: Lawrence Erlbaum.

Olsen, B. (2008) *Teaching What They Learn, Learning What They Live: How Teachers' Personal Histories Shape Their Professional Development*. Boulder, CO: Paradigm Publisher.

Pagnucci, G. (2004) *Living the Narrative Life: Stories as a Tool for Meaning Making*. Portsmouth, NH: Boynton/Cook.

Pang, V.O. (2006) Fighting the marginalization of Asian American students with caring schools: Focusing on curricular change. *Race, Ethnicity, and Education* 9 (1), 67–83.

Park, G. (2006) Unsilencing the Silenced: The Journeys of Five East Asian Women Teachers in the US TESOL Teacher Education Programs. Doctoral dissertation, University of Maryland.

Park, G. (2008) Lived pedagogies: Becoming a multi-competent ESL teacher. In J. Carmona (ed.) *Perspectives on Community College ESL: Volume 3: Faculty, Administration, and the Working Environment* (pp. 17–29). Alexandria, VA: TESOL, Inc.

Park, G. (2009) 'I listened to Korean society. I always heard that women should be this way …': The negotiation and construction of gendered identities in claiming a dominant language and race in the US. *Journal of Language, Identity, and Education* 8 (2), 174–190.

Park, G. (2010) Providing meaningful writing opportunities in the community college: The cultural and linguistic autobiographical writing project. In S. Kasten (ed.) *TESOL Classroom Practice: Writing* (pp. 61–68). Alexandria, VA: TESOL, Inc.

Park, G. (2011) Adult English language learners constructing and sharing their stories and experiences: The cultural and linguistic autobiography (CLA) writing project. *TESOL Journal* 2 (2), 156–172. doi:10.5054/tj.2011.250378.

Park, G. (2012) 'I am never afraid of being recognized as an NNES': One woman teacher's journey in claiming and embracing the NNES identity. *TESOL Quarterly* 46 (1), 127–151.

Park, G. (2013a) My autobiographical poetic rendition: An inquiry into humanizing our teacher-scholarship. *L2 Journal Special Themed Issue: L2 Writing and Personal History* 5 (1), 6–19. See http://escholarship.org/uc/item/2wx585r5 (accessed July 1, 2013).

Park, G. (2013b) 'Writing *IS* a way of knowing': Writing and identity. *ELT Journal* 67 (3), 336–345.

Park, G. (2015) Situating the discourses of privilege and marginalization in the lives of two East Asian women teachers of English. *Race, Ethnicity and Education* 18 (1), 108–133.

Park, G. and Amevuvor, J. (2015) 'If you learn about these issues, you're going to learn … more about yourself and things that you come in contact with every day': Engaging undergraduate students in meaningful literacy in a research writing course. *Journal of Pedagogic Development* 5 (2), 50–68.

Park, G. and Amevuvor, J. (2016) A MATESOL program housed in the English department: Preparing teacher scholars to meet the demands of a globalizing world. In M. Strain (ed.) *Degree of Change: The MA in English Studies* (pp. 215–233). Urbana, IL: National Council for Teachers of English.

Park, G., Rinke, C., and Mawhinney, L. (2016) Exploring the interplay of cultural capital, habitus, and field in the life histories of two West African teacher candidates. *Teacher Development: An International Journal of Teachers' Professional Development* 20 (5), 1–20.

Pasternak, M. and Bailey, K. (2004) Preparing nonnative and native English speaking teachers: Issues of professionalism and proficiency. In L. Kamhi-Stein (ed.) *Learning and Teaching from Experience: Perspectives on Nonnative English-Speaking Professionals* (pp. 155–175). Ann Arbor, MI: University of Michigan Press.

Patton, M. (1990) Qualitative interviewing. In M. Patton (ed.) *Qualitative Evaluation and Research Methods*. (pp. 277–386). Newbury, CA: Sage Publications.

Pavlenko, A. (2001). "In the world of the tradition. I was unimagined": Negotiation of identities in cross cultural autobiographies. *International Journal of Bilingualism* 5 (3), 317–344.

Pavlenko, A. (2003) 'I never knew I was a bilingual': Reimagining teacher identities in TESOL. *Journal of Language, Identity, and Education* 2 (4), 251–268.

Pavlenko, A. (2004) Gender and sexuality in foreign and second language education: Critical and feminist approaches. In B. Norton and K. Toohey (eds) *Critical Pedagogies and Language Learning* (pp. 53–71). Cambridge: The Cambridge University, Applied Linguistic Series.

Pavlenko, A. and Blackledge, A. (2004) *Negotiation of Identities in Multilingual Contexts*. Clevedon: Multilingual Matters.

Pavlenko, A., Blackledge, A., Piller, I. and Teutsch-Dwyer, M. (eds) (2001) *Multilingualism, Second Language Learning, and Gender* (Vol. 6). Berlin: Walter de Gruyter.

Pennycook, A. (1999) Introduction: Critical approaches to TESOL. *TESOL Quarterly* 33 (3), 329–348.

Peshkin, A. (1988) In search of subjectivity: One's own. *Educational Researcher* October, 17–21.

Phan, L.H. (2008) *Teaching English as an International Language: Identity, Resistance and Negotiation*. Clevedon: Multilingual Matters.

Phillipson, R. (1992) *Linguistic Imperialism*. Oxford: Oxford University Press.

Preskill, S. (1998) Narratives of teaching and the quest for the second self. *Journal of Teacher Education* 49 (5), 344–357.

Price, J. (2002) Lessons from against the odds. *Journal of Teacher Education* 53 (2), 117–126.

Ramanathan, V. (2005) Situating the researcher in research texts: Dilemmas, questions, ethics, and new directions. *Journal of Identity, Language, and Education* 4 (4), 291–293.

Reucker, T. and Ives, L. (2015) White native English speakers needed: The rhetorical construction of privilege in online teacher recruitment spaces. *TESOL Quarterly* 49 (4), 733–756.

Rinke, C., Mawhinney, L., and Park, G. (2014). The apprenticeship of observation in career contexts: A typology for the role of modeling in teachers' career paths. *Teachers and Teaching: Theory and Practice* 20 (1), 92–107.

Saft, S. and Ohara, Y. (2004) Promoting critical reflection about gender in EFL classes at a Japanese university. In B. Norton and A. Pavlenko (eds) *Gender and English Language Learners* (pp. 143–154). Alexandria, VA: TESOL.

Sharkey, J. and Johnson, K.E. (2003) *The TESOL Quarterly Dialogues: Rethinking Issues of Language, Culture, and Power*. Alexandria, VA: TESOL, Inc.

Sharma, G. (2015) Cultural schemas and pedagogical use of literacy narratives: A reflection on my journey with reading and writing. *CCC* 67 (1), 104–110.

Shin, H. (2014) Social class, habitus, and language learning: The case of Korean early study-abroad students. *Journal of Language, Identity and Education* 13, 99–103.

Shohamy, E. (2004) Reflection on research guidelines, categories, and responsibilities. *TESOL Quarterly* 30 (4), 720–730.

Shrake, E.K. (2006) Unmasking the self: Struggling with the model minority stereotype and lotus blossom image. In G. Li and H. Gulbahar (eds) *'Strangers' of the Academy: Asian Women Scholars in Higher Education* (pp. 163–177). Sterling, VA: Stylus Publisher.

Shuck, G. (2006) Racializing the nonnative English speaker. *Journal of Language, Identity, and Education* 5 (4), 259–276.

Shulman, L. (1987) Knowledge and teaching: foundations of the new reform. *Harvard Educational Review* 57 (1), 1–23.

Simon-Maeda, A. (2004) The complex construction of professional identities: Female EFL educators in Japan speak out. *TESOL Quarterly* 38 (3), 405–436.

Sinner, A. (2013) *Unfolding the Unexpectedness of Uncertainty: Creative Nonfiction and the Lives of Becoming Teachers*. Boston, MA: Sense Publishers.

Skapoulli, E. (2004) Gender codes at odds and the linguistic construction of a hybrid identity. *Journal of Language, Identity, and Education* 3 (4), 245–260.

Song, J. (2009) Language ideology and identity in transnational space: Globalization, migration, and bilingualism among Korean families in the USA. *International Journal of Bilingual Education and Bilingualism* 13 (1), 23–42.

Song, J. (2011) Globalization, children's study abroad, and transnationalism as an emerging context for language learning: A new task for language teacher education. *TESOL Quarterly* 45 (4), 749–758.

Tang, C. (1997) The identity of the nonnative ESL teacher: On the power and status of nonnative ESL teachers. *TESOL Quarterly* 31 (3), 577–583.

Toma, J. (2000) How getting close to your subjects makes qualitative data better. *Theory into Practice* 39 (3), 177–184.

Tuan, M. (2003) *Forever Foreigners or Honorary Whites?: The Asian Ethnic Experience Today*. New Brunswick, NJ: Rutgers University Press.
Turner, J.D. (2003) To tell a new story: A narrative inquiry into the theory and practice of culturally relevant teaching. Unpublished doctoral dissertation, Michigan State University.
Valian, V. (2005). Beyond gender schemas: Improving the advancement of women in academia. *Hypatia* 20 (3), 198–213.
Vandrick, S. (1995) Privilege ESL university students. *TESOL Quarterly* 29 (2), 375–381.
Vandrick, S. (2009) *Interrogating Privilege: Reflections of a Second Language Educator*. Ann Arbor, MI: University of Michigan Press.
Vandrick, S. (2011). Students of the new global elite. *TESOL Quarterly* 45 (1), 160–169.
Vandrick, S. (2014) The role of social class in English language education. *Journal of Language, Identity and Education* 13, 85–91.
Van Manan, J. (1988) *Tales of the Field: On Writing Ethnography*. Chicago, IL: The University of Chicago Press.
Van Manen, M. (1990) *Researching Lived Experience: Human Science for an Action Sensitive Pedagogy*. New York: The State University of New York.
Varghese, M., Morgan, B., Johnston, B. and Johnson, K.A. (2005) Theorizing language teacher identity: Three perspectives and beyond. *Journal of language, Identity, and Education* 4 (1), 21–44.
Varghese, M., Motha, S., Park, G., Trent, X. and Reeves, X. (2016) Language teacher identity in (multi)lingual educational contexts. *TESOL Quarterly* special issue.
Viete, R. and Ha, P.L. (2007) The growth of voice: Expanding possibilities for representing self in research writing. *English Teaching: Practice and Critique* 6 (2), 39–57.
Vitanova, G. (2004) Gender enactments in immigrants' discursive practices: Bringing Bakhtin to the dialogue. *Journal of Language, Identity, and Education* 3 (4), 261–277.
Warriner, D. (2004) "The days now is very hard for my family": The negotiation and construction of gendered work identities among newly arrived women refugees. *Journal of Language, Identity, and Education* 3 (4), 279–294.
Weedon, C. (1987) *Feminist Practice and Poststructuralist Theory*. Oxford: Basil Blackwell.
Weinstein, G. (2004) Immigrant adults and their teachers: Community and professional development through family literacy. *The CATESOL Journal* 16 (1), 111–124.
Weinstein, D. and Park, G. (2014) Helping students connect: Architecting learning spaces for experiential and transactional reflection. *Journal of Pedagogic Development* 4 (3), 14–22.
Wenger, E. (1998) *Communities of Practice: Learning, Meaning, and Identity*. Cambridge: Cambridge University Press.
Widdowson, H.G. (1994) The ownership of English. *TESOL Quarterly* 28, 377–389.
Yoon, S. (2014) The Qualifications for Being and Becoming English Language Teachers Across Junior/High School Level Public and Private Schools in South Korea. Unpublished thesis, Indiana University of Pennsylvania.

Index

Agency 1, 98–99
Autobiography xviii, xxv, 1–2, 30, 35, 37, 108
    Autobiographical Poetic Inquiry 1
    Autobiographical Poetic Waves 3–4, 6–7
    Autobiographical Self xxiv, 29–31

Bilingual (Identity) 6, 36, 53–55, 76, 88–89

Capital (Bourdieu) xix, 15, 17, 74
    Context Specific 19
    Cultural 16, 19, 61, 85
    Economic 18
    Human 20
    Linguistic 4, 16
    Social 16, 18, 61, 85
    Symbolic 11, 16, 19, 41
Critical Incidents xxvi, 3, 37, 94–95, 100–103
Educational Incidents 107
(Dis)Connectedness xviii, xix
Discoursal self 29–30
(Dis)Empowerment 62, 85
Disposition 16, 34

English as an Additional Language (EAL) xvii–xviii, xxiii, 2, 4, 26
English as an International Language (EIL) xxiii, 5
Englishization xxi
Ethnicity x, 5, 16, 21, 32, 36, 40
Expanding Circle Countries (ECC) 23–25

Feminist ix, 13, 14, 58

Gender(ed) xx, xxii, xxiv, xxv, 3, 7, 11, 14–16, 21–22, 27, 31–32, 36, 40, 43, 48
    Gendered Experience xiv, 48
    Gendered Research Experience xiv
    Lesser Gender 5
    Inferior Gender 6

Race-gender-social class connection 11, 13, 27, 28
    Position 45
    Equity 45, 47
    Desire 45
    Responsibilities 51
    Access 51
    Practices 52
Gerogi Gajok (geese family) 4

Identity
    Bicultural 5
    Class (Social Class) xix, xxii, 11, 16, 18, 21–22, 32
    (de)/(re)constructed xxi, 16
    (Dis)empowered 68
    Fluid xiii, xx, 7, 13, 42, 58, 102
    Gender xxi, xxv, 13, 37, 44–45, 47, 51–51, 53
    Imagined xx, xxii, 39, 45, 50, 56, 58–59, 61, 92–93
    Language Teacher or Teacher xvii, xxiv, 2, 7, 11–12, 14, 27, 33, 45, 52, 54–55, 78, 87, 92
    Linguistic xviii, xxi, xxv, 3, 7, 12, 15, 17, 31, 37, 43, 49, 53–55, 61–61, 65, 69, 70, 74, 85–86
    Mothering xxii, 45, 52–53, 55, 102
    Multilingual xxiv, 7, 61, 65, 68, 76, 79–80, 85, 90, 101
    Multiple xiii, xxii, xxiii, xxv, 3, 13–14, 42, 44,
    Professional xxii, 3, 33, 43, 52–53, 55–58, 88, 92
    Racial 3, 6, 7, 16–17, 31, 37, 49–50, 54–55, 65, 70, 85, 94, 97
    Socially Constructed 29
    Transnational xx, xxiv, 6, 15, 19, 24, 54
Ideology xx, xxiii, 35, 87
    Achievement 21–22
    Dominant 17, 32, 39
    Native Speaker(ist)/Nativist 15, 85
Inner Circle Countries (ICCs) 23–25

Index

Linguistic
  Powerlessness xv
  Resources xvii, 51
  Context xx, 7, 13
  Privilege and marginalization xxi, xxiii, 16, 50
  Repertoire xxiii
  Expression 2
  Broker 5
  Experiences 62
  Competence 24
  Code 31
  Structure 72
  Complexity 73
  Barriers 73
  Collegiality 76
  Backgrounds 91
  Proficiency 91
  Choices 94
  Minorities 97
  Issues 103
Instrumentalism 20
Lived Experiences xiii, xvii, xx, xxii–xxiii, xxv, 1, 3, 6, 7, 9, 13, 15, 19, 30–33, 36, 38, 42, 44–45, 51, 58, 87–88, 96

Mama Scholar xxi, xxiii, xxv, xxvi, 9, 38, 45
  Mama Ph.D 7–8
  Mama Teacher Scholar 38
Marginalization xiii, xix, xxi–xxvi, 3, 11–14, 17–18, 20, 22, 31, 38, 42–44, 60, 62, 68, 74, 86, 94–95, 100, 102
  Self-perceived Marginalization 8
  Gendered marginalization 50
Meaningful Literacy 3, 36
Meta-Awareness 24
Minority xxi–xxii, 3, 102
  Model Minority 21–22
  Visible Minority 3–4, 7, 14–16, 53–54, 89

Narratives xxiv–xxvi, 13, 34, 41–42, 47, 58, 60, 95, 102–104
  Autobiographical xxvi
  Personal xiii, 37, 42, 95
  Teacher Identity xix
  Women's xxii, xxvi, 41, 94
  Constructed 1
  Life history 31, 35
  Master 33, 102
  Symbolic 33
  Sacred 33
  Scientific 33
  Literacy 34
  Grand 38, 42
  Student 97
  Critical incident 102
Nonnative English Speaker (NNES) xvi–xvii, xix–xx, 4, 6–7, 14, 42, 54, 60–61, 69–70, 72–74, 76–77, 79–80, 84–85, 88–89, 91–92
  Near-NNES xx, xxiii
  Native English Speaker (NES) xxiii
  Nonnative English speaking teachers 16–17, 20, 22–23, 25, 39, 78
  Nonnative English Speaking Professionals 18

Othered 70, 101
Outer Circle Countries (OCCs) 23–25

Pedagogy xvii, 1, 7, 25, 30, 57, 79–81, 89–91, 109
  Critical 26
  Postmethod 27
Power xxi, xxv, xxvi, 1, 6, 11, 15, 17, 19, 23–24, 36, 412, 45, 50, 60, 69, 95, 101–102
Privilege xiii, xix, xxi–xxvi, 1, 3, 7, 11–18, 20, 22, 24, 27, 31–33, 35, 38–40, 42–45, 60–61, 68, 74, 85, 94–96, 100, 102–103
  White Privilege 3, 12, 17

Race x, xxii, xxiv, 3, 7, 11, 13, 15–17, 22, 27, 31–32, 38–40, 43, 50, 58, 76, 85–86, 100–103
Racial
  Racialized discourses xxiv, 15
  Climate 5
  Context(s) 7
  Marginalization 16, 50
  Hierarchy 21
  Inequalities 21
  Groupings 89
  Epistemologies 102
Researcher Subjectivity xx, xxiv

Self xiii, 16–17, 25, 31, 40
  Autobiographical self xxiv, 29–31

Women of Color xxv, 14, 86, 95, 102

For Product Safety Concerns and Information please contact our EU Authorised Representative:

Easy Access System Europe

Mustamäe tee 50

10621 Tallinn

Estonia

gpsr.requests@easproject.com